EDUCATION : DESIGNING AND BUILDING OUR COMMON FUTURE

EDUCATION :
Designing and Building our Common Future

Editor

Prof. Ramesh Chandra

Publications

KALPAZ PUBLICATIONS

DELHI-110052

EDUCATION : DESIGNING AND BUILDING OUR COMMON FUTURE

Education : Designing and Building
our Common Future

Rs. 575

ISBN: 81-7835-230-3

This book is Vol. No. 2 of Universal Education and Technology in 21st Century (Set)

Published in 2005 in India by
Kalpaz Publications,
C-30, Satyawati Nagar, Delhi-110052
E-mail : Kalpaz@hotmail.com

Laser Typesetting at : Master Computers, Delhi
Printed at : Ajit Printers, Delhi

Contents

Preface

Education is the critical force in creating tolerance, respect for diversity and peaceful understanding—a purpose which has gained even more significance in light of recent developments on the world scene. It is central to the current, pervasive emphasis to establish a mutually reinforcing relationship between macro-economic stability and structural reform on one hand, and growth and reduction of poverty and inequality on the other. It is the key to participation in the global economy of the 21st century, based on technological revolutions in communications and transfer of information, as well as major changes in production, transport and distribution, and the economic value of knowledge.

All governments have a responsibility to fulfil their human rights obligation to provide, free and compulsory basic education of good quality for all children, especially girls, youth, immigrants, indigenous students, children with special needs or in difficult circumstances and those belonging to ethnic minorities, in accordance with the commitment made in the Dakar Framework for Action by 2015. In today's world, the mission of quality public schooling is not limited to the basic years of education, but includes secondary school and the acquisition of vocational qualifications.

The 21 century represents growth in the area of technology and human development. In order to fulfil the requirements of the new age successfully, all nations must determine the extent to which their educational systems are preparing the next generation for successful participation in the existing enterprise. For this it is essential to understand the requirements, possibilities and problems of a country, and prepare an alternative plan based on the challenges of the new millennium.

For the new era skill-based learning should be emphasised. Learning should be based on hardware and software. There will be global thinking in education. The teacher should be fully acquainted with the different teaching skills and they can use them successfully in the classrooms. In the education process continuous improvement should be achieved through different methods of learning theory and practical aspects should be interlinked and enriched by experiments and innovations. Time to time a systematic evaluation should be done to know the achievements of students, institutions and teachers.

Editor

1

World Declaration on Education for All

PREAMBLE

More than 40 years ago, the nations of the world, speaking through the Universal Declaration of Human Rights, asserted that "everyone has a right to education". Despite notable efforts by countries around the globe to ensure the right to education for all, the following realities persist:

More than 100 million children, including at least 60 million girls, have no access to primary schooling;

More than 960 million adults, two-thirds of whom are women, are illiterate, and functional illiteracy is a significant problem in all countries, industrialized and developing;

More than one-third of the world's adults have no access to the printed knowledge, new skills and technologies that could improve the quality of their lives and help them shape, and adapt to, social and cultural change; and

More than 100 million children and countless adults fail to complete basic education programmes; millions more satisfy the attendance requirements but do not acquire essential knowledge and skills;

At the same time, the world faces daunting problems: notably mounting debt burdens, the threat of economic stagnation and decline, rapid population growth, widening economic disparities among and within nations, war, occupation, civil strife, violent crime, the preventable deaths of millions of children and widespread environmental degradation. These problems constrain efforts to meet basic learning needs, while the lack of basic education among a significant proportion of the population prevents societies from addressing such problems with strength and purpose.

These problems have led to major setbacks in basic education in the 1980s in many of the least developed countries. In some other countries, economic growth has been available to finance education expansion, but even so, many millions remain in poverty and unschooled or illiterate. In certain industrialized countries too, cutbacks in government expenditure over the 1980s have led to the deterioration of education.

Yet the world is also at the threshold of a new century, with all its promise and possibilities. Today, there is genuine progress toward peaceful detente and greater cooperation among nations. Today, the essential rights and capacities of women are being realized. Today, there are many useful scientific and cultural developments. Today, the sheer quantity of information available in the world - much of it relevant to survival and basic well-being - is exponentially greater than that available only a few years ago, and the rate of its growth is accelerating. This includes information about obtaining more life-enhancing knowledge - or learning how to learn. A synergistic effect occurs when important information is coupled with another modern advance - our new capacity to communicate.

These new forces, when combined with the cumulative experience of reform, innovation, research and the remarkable educational progress of many countries, make the goal of basic education for all - for the first time in history - an attainable goal.

Therefore, we participants in the World Conference on Education for All, assembled in Jomtien, Thailand, from 5 to 9 March, 1990:

Recalling that education is a fundamental right for all people, women and men, of all ages, throughout our world;

Understanding that education can help ensure a safer, healthier, more prosperous and environmentally sound world, while simultaneously contributing to social, economic, and cultural progress, tolerance, and international cooperation;

Knowing that education is an indispensable key to, though not a sufficient condition for, personal and social improvement;

Recognizing that traditional knowledge and indigenous cultural heritage have a value and validity in their own right and a capacity to both define and promote development;

Acknowledging that, overall, the current provision of education is seriously deficient and that it must be made more relevant and qualitatively improved, and made universally available:

Recognizing that sound basic education is fundamental to the strengthening of higher levels of education and of scientific and technological literacy and capacity and thus to self-reliant development; and

Recognizing the necessity to give to present and coming generations an expanded vision of, and a renewed commitment to, basic education to address the scale and complexity of the challenge; proclaim the following:

EDUCATION FOR ALL: THE PURPOSE

ARTICLE I - MEETING BASIC LEARNING NEEDS

1. Every person - child, youth and adult - shall be able to benefit from educational opportunities designed to meet their basic learning needs. These needs comprise both essential learning tools (such as literacy, oral expression, numeracy, and problem solving) and the basic learning content (such as knowledge, skills, values, and attitudes) required by human beings to be able to survive, to develop their full capacities, to live and work in dignity, to participate fully in development, to improve the quality of their lives, to make informed decisions, and to continue learning. The scope of basic learning needs and how they should be met varies with individual countries and cultures, and inevitably, changes with the passage of time.

2. The satisfaction of these needs empowers individuals in any society and confers upon them a responsibility to respect and build upon their collective cultural, linguistic and spiritual heritage, to promote the

education of others, to further the cause of social justice, to achieve environmental protection, to be tolerant towards social, political and religious systems which differ from their own, ensuring that commonly accepted humanistic values and human rights are upheld, and to work for international peace and solidarity in an interdependent world.

3. Another and no less fundamental aim of educational development is the transmission and enrichment of common cultural and moral values. It is in these values that the individual and society find their identity and worth.

4. Basic education is more than an end in itself. It is the foundation for lifelong learning and human development on which countries may build, systematically, further levels and types of education and training.

EDUCATION FOR ALL: AN EXPANDED VISION AND A RENEWED COMMITMENT

ARTICLE II - SHAPING THE VISION

To serve the basic learning needs of all requires more than a recommitment to basic education as it now exists. What is needed is an "expanded vision" that surpasses present resource levels, institutional structures, curricula, and conventional delivery systems while building on the best in current practices. New possibilities exist today which result from the convergence of the increase in information and the unprecedented capacity to communicate. We must seize them with creativity and a determination for increased effectiveness.

As elaborated in Articles III-VII, the expanded vision encompasses:

— Universalizing access and promoting equity;

— Focussing on learning;

— Broadening the means and scope of basic education;

— Enhancing the environment for learning;

— Strengthening partnerships.

The realization of an enormous potential for human progress and empowerment is contingent upon whether people can be enabled to acquire the education and the start needed to tap into the ever-expanding pool of relevant knowledge and the new means for sharing this knowledge.

ARTICLE III - UNIVERSALIZING ACCESS AND PROMOTING EQUITY

1. Basic education should be provided to all children, youth and adults. To this end, basic education services of quality should be expanded and consistent measures must be taken to reduce disparities.

2. For basic education to be equitable, all children, youth and adults must be given the opportunity to achieve and maintain an acceptable level of learning.

3. The most urgent priority is to ensure access to, and improve the quality of, education for girls and women, and to remove every obstacle that hampers their active participation. All gender stereotyping in education should be eliminated.

4. An active commitment must be made to removing educational disparities. Underserved groups: the poor; street and working children; rural and remote populations; nomads and migrant workers; indigenous peoples; ethnic, racial, and linguistic minorities; refugees; those displaced by war; and people under occupation, should not suffer any discrimination in access to learning opportunities.
5. The learning needs of the disabled demand special attention. Steps need to be taken to provide equal access to education to every category of disabled persons as an integral part of the education system.

ARTICLE IV - FOCUSSING ON LEARNING

Whether or not expanded educational opportunities will translate into meaningful development - for an individual or for society - depends ultimately on whether people actually learn as a result of those opportunities, i.e., whether they incorporate useful knowledge, reasoning ability, skills, and values. The focus of basic education must, therefore, be on actual learning acquisition and outcome, rather than exclusively upon enrolment, continued participation in organized programmes and completion of certification requirements. Active and participatory approaches are particularly valuable in assuring learning acquisition and allowing learners to reach their fullest potential. It is, therefore, necessary to define acceptable levels of learning acquisition for educational programmes and to improve and apply systems of assessing learning achievement.

ARTICLE V - BROADENING THE MEANS AND SCOPE OF BASIC EDUCATION

The diversity, complexity, and changing nature of basic learning needs of children, youth and adults necessitates broadening and constantly redefining the scope of basic education to include the following components:

Learning begins at birth. This calls for early childhood care and initial education. These can be provided through arrangements involving families, communities, or institutional programmes, as appropriate.

The main delivery system for the basic education of children outside the family is primary schooling. Primary education must be universal, ensure that the basic learning needs of all children are satisfied, and take into account the culture, needs, and opportunities of the community. Supplementary alternative programmes can help meet the basic learning needs of children with limited or no access to formal schooling, provided that they share the same standards of learning applied to schools, and are adequately supported.

The basic learning needs of youth and adults are diverse and should be met through a variety of delivery systems. Literacy programmes are indispensable because literacy is a necessary skill in itself and the foundation of other life skills. Literacy in the mother-tongue strengthens cultural identity and heritage. Other needs can be served by: skills training, apprenticeships, and formal and non-formal education programmes in health, nutrition, population, agricultural techniques, the environment, science, technology, family life, including fertility awareness, and other societal issues.

All available instruments and channels of information, communications, and social action could be used to help convey essential knowledge and inform and educate people on social issues. In addition to the traditional means, libraries, television, radio and other media can be mobilized to realize their potential towards meeting basic education needs of all.

These components should constitute an integrated system - complementary, mutually reinforcing, and of comparable standards, and they should contribute to creating and developing possibilities for lifelong learning.

ARTICLE VI - ENHANCING THE ENVIRONMENT FOR LEARNING

Learning does not take place in isolation. Societies, therefore, must ensure that all learners receive the nutrition, health care, and general physical and emotional support they need in order to participate actively in and benefit from their education. Knowledge and skills that will enhance the learning environment of children should be integrated into community learning programmes for adults. The education of children and their parents or other caretakers is mutually supportive and this interaction should be used to create, for all, a learning environment of vibrancy and warmth.

ARTICLE VII - STRENGTHENING PARTNERSHIPS

National, regional, and local educational authorities have a unique obligation to provide basic education for all, but they cannot be expected to supply every human, financial or organizational requirement for this task. New and revitalized partnerships at all levels will be necessary: partnerships among all sub-sectors and forms of education, recognizing the special role of teachers and that of administrators and other educational personnel; partnerships between education and other government departments, including planning, finance, labour, communications, and other social sectors; partnerships between government and non-governmental organizations, the private sector, local communities, religious groups, and families. The recognition of the vital role of both families and teachers is particularly important. In this context, the terms and conditions of service of teachers and their status, which constitute a determining factor in the implementation of education for all, must be urgently improved in all countries in line with the joint ILO/ UNESCO Recommendation Concerning the Status of Teachers (1966). Genuine partnerships contribute to the planning, implementing, managing and evaluating of basic education programmes. When we speak of "an expanded vision and a renewed commitment", partnerships are at the heart of it.

EDUCATION FOR ALL: THE REQUIREMENTS

ARTICLE VIII - DEVELOPING A SUPPORTIVE POLICY CONTEXT

1. Supportive policies in the social, cultural, and economic sectors are required in order to realize the full provision and utitlization of basic education for individual and societal improvement. The provision of basic education for all depends on political commitment and political will backed by appropriate fiscal measures and reinforced by educational policy

reforms and institutional strengthening. Suitable economic, trade, labour, employment and health policies will enhance learners' incentives and contributions to societal development.

2. Societies should also insure a strong intellectual and scientific environment for basic education. This implies improving higher education and developing scientific research. Close contact with contemporary technological and scientific knowledge should be possible at every level of education.

ARTICLE IX - MOBILIZING RESOURCES

1. If the basic learning needs of all are to be met through a much broader scope of action than in the past, it will be essential to mobilize existing and new financial and human resources, public, private and voluntary. All of society has a contribution to make, recognizing that time, energy and funding directed to basic education are perhaps the most profound investment in people and in the future of a country which can be made.

2. Enlarged public-sector support means drawing on the resources of all the government agencies responsible for human development, through increased absolute and proportional allocations to basic education services with the clear recognition of competing claims on national resources of which education is an important one, but not the only one. Serious attention to improving the efficiency of existing educational resources and programmes will not only produce more, it can also be expected to attract new resources. The urgent task of meeting basic learning needs may

require a reallocation between sectors, as, for example, a transfer from military to educational expenditure. Above all, special protection for basic education will be required in countries undergoing structural adjustment and facing severe external debt burdens. Today, more than ever, education must be seen as a fundamental dimension of any social, cultural, and economic design.

ARTICLE X - STRENGTHENING INTERNATIONAL SOLIDARITY

1. Meeting basic learning needs constitutes a common and universal human responsibility. It requires international solidarity and equitable and fair economic relations in order to redress existing economic disparities. All nations have valuable knowledge and experiences to share for designing effective educational policies and programmes.

2. Substantial and long-term increases in resources for basic education will be needed. The world community, including intergovernmental agencies and institutions, has an urgent responsibility to alleviate the constraints that prevent some countries from achieving the goal of education for all. It will mean the adoption of measures that augment the national budgets of the poorest countries or serve to relieve heavy debt burdens. Creditors and debtors must seek innovative and equitable formulae to resolve these burdens, since the capacity of many developing countries to respond effectively to education and other basic needs will be greatly helped by finding solutions to the debt problem.

3. Basic learning needs of adults and children must be addressed wherever they exist. Least developed and low-income countries have special needs which require priority in international support for basic education in the 1990s.

4. All nations must also work together to resolve conflicts and strife, to end military occupations, and to settle displaced populations, or to facilitate their return to their countries of origin, and ensure that their basic learning needs are met. Only a stable and peaceful environment can create the conditions in which every human being, child and adult alike, may benefit from the goals of this Declaration.

We, the participants in the World Conference on Education for All, reaffirm the right of all people to education. This is the foundation of our determination, singly and together, to ensure education for all. We commit ourselves to act cooperatively through our own spheres of responsibility, taking all necessary steps to achieve the goals of education for all. Together we call on governments, concerned organizations and individuals to join in this urgent undertaking. The basic learning needs of all can and must be met. There can be no more meaningful way to begin the International Literacy Year, to move forward the goals of the United Nations Decade of Disabled Persons (1983-92), the World Decade for Cultural Development (1988-97), the Fourth United Nations Development Decade (1991-2000), of the Convention on the Elimination of Discrimination against Women and the Forward Looking Strategies for the Advancement of Women, and of the Convention on the Rights of the Child. There has never been a more propitious time to commit ourselves to providing basic learning opportunities for all the people of the world. We adopt, therefore, this World Declaration on Education for All: Meeting Basic Learning Needs and agree on the Framework for Action to Meet Basic Learning Needs, to achieve the goals set forth in this Declaration.

Guidelines for Implementing the World Declaration on Education for All

INTRODUCTION

This Framework for Action to Meet Basic Learning Needs derives from the World Declaration on Education for All, adopted by the World Conference on Education for All, which brought together representatives of governments, international and bilateral development agencies, and non-governmental organizations. Based on the best collective knowledge and the commitment of these partners, the Framework is intended as a reference and guide for national governments, international organizations, bilateral aid agencies, non-governmental organizations (NGOs), and all those committed to the goal of Education for All in formulating their own plans of action for implementing the World Declaration. It describes three broad levels of concerted action:

— direct action within individual countries,

— co-operation among groups of countries sharing certain characteristics and concerns, and

— multilateral and bilateral co-operation in the world community.

Individual countries and groups of countries, as well as international, regional and national organizations, may use the Framework to develop their own specific plans of action and programmes in line with their particular objectives, mandates and constituencies. This indeed has been the case in the ten-year experience of the UNESCO Major Project on Education for Latin America and the Caribbean. Further examples of such related initiatives are the UNESCO Plan of Action for the Eradication of Illiteracy by the Year 2000, adopted by the UNESCO General Conference at its 25th session (1989); the ISESCO Special Programme (1990); the current review by the World Bank of its policy for primary education; and USAID's programme for Advancing Basic Education and Literacy. Insofar as such plans of action, policies and programmes are consistent with this Framework, efforts throughout the world to meet basic learning needs will converge and facilitate co-operation. While countries have many common concerns in meeting the basic learning needs of their populations, these concerns do, of course, vary in nature and intensity from country to country depending on the actual status of basic education as well as the cultural and socio-economic context. Globally by the year 2000, if enrolment rates remain at current levels, there will be more than 160 million children without access to primary schooling simply because of population growth. In much of sub-Saharan Africa and in many low income countries elsewhere, the provision of universal primary education for rapidly growing numbers of children remains a long-term challenge. Despite progress in promoting adult literacy, most of these same countries still have high illiteracy rates, while the numbers of functionally illiterate adults continue to grow and constitute a major social problem in much of Asia and the Arab States, as well as in Europe and North America. Many people are denied equal access on grounds of race, gender, language, disability, ethnic origin, or political convictions. In addition, high drop-out rates and poor learning achievement are commonly recognized problems throughout the world. These very general characterizations illustrate the need for decisive action on a large scale, with clear goals and targets.

GOALS AND TARGETS

The ultimate goal affirmed by the World Declaration on Education for All is to meet the basic learning needs of all children, youth, and adults. The long-term effort to attain that goal can be maintained more effectively if intermediate goals are established and progress toward these goals is measured. Appropriate authorities at the national and subnational levels may establish such intermediate goals, taking into account the objectives of the Declaration as well as overall national development goals and priorities. Intermediate goals can usefully be formulated as specific targets within national and subnational plans for educational development. Such targets usually

1. specify expected attainments and outcomes in reference to terminal performance specifications within an appropriate time-frame,
2. specify priority categories (e. g. the poor, the disabled), and
3. are formulated in terms such that progress toward them can be observed and measured. These targets represent a "floor" (but not a "ceiling") for the continued development of education programmes and services.

Time-bound targets convey a sense of urgency and serve as a reference against which indices of implementation and accomplishment can be compared. As societal conditions change, plans and targets can be reviewed and updated. Where basic education efforts must be focussed to meet the needs of specific social groups or population categories, linking targets to such priority categories of learners can help to maintain the attention of planners, practitioners and evaluators on meeting the needs of these learners. Observable and measurable targets assist in the objective evaluation of progress. Targets need not be based solely on current trends and resources. Initial targets can reflect a realistic appraisal of the possibilities presented by the Declaration to mobilize additional human, organizational, and financial capacities within a cooperative commitment to human development. Countries with low literacy and school enrolment rates, and very limited national resources, will need to make hard choices in establishing national targets within a realistic timeframe.

Countries may wish to set their own targets for the 1990s in terms of the following proposed dimensions:

1. Expansion of early childhood care and developmental activities, including family and community interventions, especially for poor, disadvantaged and disabled children;

2. Universal access to, and completion of, primary education (or whatever higher level of education is considered as "basic") by the year 2000;

3. Improvement in learning achievement such that an agreed percentage of an appropriate age cohort (e. g. 80% of 14 year-olds) attains or surpasses a defined level of necessary learning achievement;

4. Reduction of the adult illiteracy rate (the appropriate age group to be determined in each country) to, say,

one-half its 1990 level by the year 2000, with sufficient emphasis on female literacy to significantly reduce the current disparity between male and female illiteracy rates;

5. Expansion of provisions of basic education and training in other essential skills required by youth and adults, with programme effectiveness assessed in terms of behavioural changes and impacts on health, employment and productivity;
6. Increased acquisition by individuals and families of the knowledge, skills and values required for better living and sound and sustainable development, made available through all education channels including the mass media, other forms of modern and traditional communication, and social action, with effectiveness assessed in terms of behavioural change.

Levels of performance in the above should be established, when possible. These should be consistent with the focus of basic education both on universalization of access and on learning acquisition, as joint and inseparable concerns. In all cases, the performance targets should include equity by gender. However, setting levels of performance and of the proportions of participants who are expected to reach these levels in specific basic education programmes must be an autonomous task of individual countries.

PRINCIPLES OF ACTION

The first step consists in identifying, preferably through an active participatory process involving groups and the community, the traditional learning systems which exist in the society, and the actual demand for basic education services, whether expressed in terms of formal schooling or non-formal education programmes. Addressing the basic learning needs of all means: early childhood care and development opportunities; relevant, quality primary schooling or equivalent out-of-school education for children; and literacy, basic knowledge and life skills training for youth and adults. It also means capitalizing on the use of traditional and modern information media and technologies to educate the public on matters of social concern and to support basic education activities. These complementary components of basic education need to be designed to ensure equitable access, sustained participation, and effective learning achievement. Meeting basic learning needs also involves action to enhance the family and community environments for learning and to correlate basic education and the larger socio-economic context. The complementarity and synergistic effects of related human resources investments in population, health and nutrition should be recognized.

Because basic learning needs are complex and diverse, meeting them requires multisectoral strategies and action wh ich are integral to overall development efforts. Many partners must join with the education authorities, teachers, and other educational personnel in developing basic education if it is to be seen, once again, as the responsibility of the entire society. This implies the active involvement of a wide range of partners

— families, teachers, communities, private enterprises (including those involved in information and communication), government and non-governmental organizations, institutions, etc.

— in planning, managing and evaluating the many forms of basic education. Current practices and institutional arrangements for delivering basic education, and the existing mechanisms for co-operation in this regard, should be carefully evaluated before new institutions or mechanisms are created. Rehabilitating dilapidated schools and improving the training and working conditions of teachers and literacy workers, building on existing learning schemes, are likely to bring greater and more immediate returns on investment than attempts to start afresh.

Great potential lies in possible joint actions with non-governmental organizations on all levels. These autonomous bodies, while advocating independent and critical public views, might play roles in monitoring, research, training and material production for the sake of non-formal and life-long educational processes.

The primary purpose of bilateral and multilateral co-operation should appear in a true spirit of partnership - it should not be to transplant familiar models, but to help develop the endogenous capacities of national authorities and their in-country partners to meet basic learning needs effectively. Action and resources should be used to strengthen essential features of basic education services, focussing on managerial and analytical capacities, which can stimulate further developments. International co-operation and funding can be particularly valuable in supporting major reforms or sectoral adjustments, and in helping to develop and test innovative approaches to teaching and management, where new approaches need to be tried and/or extraordinary levels of expenditure are involved and where knowledge of relevant experiences elsewhere can often be useful.

International co-operation should give priority to the countries currently least able to meet the basic learning needs of their populations. It should also help countries redress their internal disparities in educational opportunity. Because two-thirds of illiterate adults and out-of-school children are female, wherever such inequities exist, a most urgent priority is to improve access to education for girls and women, and to remove every obstacle that hampers their active participation.

I. Priority Action at National Level

Progress in meeting the basic learning needs of all will depend ultimately on the actions taken within individual countries. While regional and international co-operation and financial assistance can support and facilitate such actions, government authorities, communities and their several in-country partners are the key agents for improvement, and national governments have the main responsibility for coordinating the effective use of internal and external resources. Given the diversity of countries' situations, capacities and development plans and goals, this Framework can only suggest certain areas that merit priority attention. Each country will determine for itself what specific actions beyond current efforts may be necessary in each of the following areas.

1 Assessing Needs and Planning Action

To achieve the targets set for itself, each country is encouraged to develop or update comprehensive and long-term plans of action (from local to national levels) to meet the learning needs it has defined as "basic". Within the context of existing education-sector and general development plans and strategies, a plan of action for basic education for all will necessarily be multisectoral, to guide activities in the sectors involved (e. g. education, information, communications/ media, labour, agriculture, health). Models of strategic planning, by definition, vary. However, most of them involve constant adjustments among objectives, resources, actions, and constraints. At the national level, objectives are normally couched in broad terms and central government resources are also determined, while actions are taken at the local level. Thus, local plans in the same national setting will naturally differ not only in scope but in content. National and subnational frameworks and local plans should allow for varying conditions and circumstances. These might, therefore, specify:

— studies for the evaluation of existing systems (analysis of problems, failures and successes):

— the basic learning needs to be met, including cognitive skills, values, attitudes, as well as subject knowledge;

— the languages to be used in education

— means to promote the demand for, and broadscale participation in, basic education;

— modalities to mobilize family and local community support;

— targets and specific objectives;

— the required capital and recurrent resources, duly costed, as well as possible measures for cost effectiveness;

— indicators and procedures to be used to monitor progress in reaching the targets;

— priorities for using resources and for developing services and programmes over time;

— the priority groups that require special measures;

— the kinds of expertise required to implement the plan;

— institutional and administrative arrangements needed;

— modalities for ensuring information sharing among formal and other basic education programmes; and

— an implementation strategy and timetable.

2 *Developing a Supportive Policy Environment*

A multisectoral plan of action implies adjustments to sectoral policies so that sectors interact in a mutually supportive and beneficial manner in line with the country's overall development goals. Action to meet basic learning needs should be an integral part of a country's national and subnational development strategies, which should reflect the priority given to human development. Legislative and other measures may be needed to promote and facilitate co-operation among the various partners involved. Advocacy and public information about basic education are important in creating a supportive policy environment at national, subnational and local levels.

Four specific steps that merit attention are:

1. initiation of national and subnational level activities to create a broad, public recommitment to the goal of education for all;

2. reduction of inefficiency in the public sector and exploitative practices in the private sector;
3. provision of improved training for public administrators and of incentives to retain qualified women and men in public service; and
4. provision of measures to encourage wider participation in the design and implementation of basic education programmes.

3 Designing Policies to Improve Basic Education

The preconditions for educational quality, equity and efficiency, are set in the early childhood years, making attention to early childhood care and development essential to the achievement of basic education goals. Basic education must correspond to actual needs, interests, and problems of the participants in the learning process. The relevance of curricula could be enhanced by linking literacy and numeracy skills and scientific concepts with learners' concerns and earlier experiences, for example, nutrition, health, and work. While many needs vary considerably within and among countries, and therefore much of a curriculum should be sensitive to local conditions, there are also many universal needs and shared concerns which should be addressed in education curricula and in educational messages. Issues such as protecting the environment, achieving a balance between population and resources, slowing the spread of AIDS, and preventing drug abuse are everyone's issues.

Specific strategies addressed to improve the conditions of schooling may focus on: learners and the learning process, personnel (teachers, administrators, others), curriculum and learning assessment, materials and physical facilities. Such strategies should be conducted in an integrated manner; their design, management, and evaluation should take into account the acquisition of knowledge and problem-solving skills as well as the social, cultural, and ethical dimensions of human development. Depending on the outcomes desired, teachers have to be trained accordingly, whilst benefiting from in-service programmes as well as other incentives of opportunity which put a premium on the achievement of these outcomes; curriculum and assessment must reflect a variety of criteria while materials - and conceivably buildings and facilities as well - must be adapted along the same lines. In some countries, the strategy may include ways to improve conditions for teaching and learning such that absenteeism is reduced and learning time increased. In order to meet the educational needs of groups not covered by formal schooling, appropriate strategies are needed for non-formal education. These include but go far beyond the aspects described above, but may also give special attention to the need for coordination with other forms of education, to the support of all interested partners, to sustained financial resources and to full community participation. An example for such an approach applied to literacy can be found in UNESCO's Plan of Action for the Eradication of Illiteracy by the Year 2000. Other strategies still may rely on the media to meet the broader education needs of the entire community. Such strategies need to be linked to formal education, non-formal education or a combination of both. The use of the communications media holds a tremendous potential to educate the public and to share important information among those who need to know.

Expanding access to basic education of satisfactory quality is an effective way to improve equity. Ensuring that girls and women stay involved in basic education activities until they have attained at least the agreed necessary level of learning, can be encouraged through special measures designed, wherever possible, in consultation with them. Similar approaches are necessary to expand learning opportunities for various disadvantaged groups.

Efficiency in basic education does not mean providing education at the lowest cost, but rather the most effective use of all resources (human, organizational, and financial) to produce the desired levels of access and of necessary learning achievement. The foregoing considerations of relevance, quality, and equity are not alternatives to efficiency but represent the specific conditions within which efficiency should be attained. For some programmes, efficiency will require more, not fewer, resources. However, if existing resources can be used by more learners or if the same learning targets can be reached at a lower cost per learner, then the capacity of basic education to meet the targets of access and achievement for presently underserved groups can be increased.

4 Improving Managerial, Analytical and Technological Capacities

Many kinds of expertise and skills will be needed to carry out these initiatives. Managerial and supervisory personnel, as well as planners, school architects, teacher educators, curriculum developers, researchers, analysts, etc., are important for any strategy to improve basic education, but many countries do not provide specialized training to prepare them for their responsibilities; this is especially true in literacy and other out-of-school basic education activities. A broadening of outlook toward basic education will be a crucial prerequisite to the effective co-ordination of efforts among these many participants, and strengthening and developing capacities for planning and management at regional and local levels with a greater sharing of responsibilities will be necessary in many countries. Pre- and in-service training programmes for key personnel should be initiated, or strengthened where they do exist. Such training can be particularly useful in introducing administrative reforms and innovative management and supervisory techniques.

The technical services and mechanisms to collect, process and analyze data pertaining to basic education can be improved in all countries. This is an urgent task in many countries that have little reliable information and/or research on the basic learning needs of their people and on existing basic education activities. A country's information and knowledge base is vital in preparing and implementing a plan of action. One major implication of the focus on learning acquisition is that systems have to be developed and improved to assess the performance of individual learners and delivery mechanisms. Process and outcome assessment data should serve as the core of a management information system for basic education. The quality and delivery of basic education can be enhanced through the judicious use of instructional technologies. Where such technologies are not now widely used, their introduction will require the selection and/or development of suitable technologies, acquisition of the necessary equipment and operating systems, and the recruitment or training of teachers and other educational personnel to work with them. The definition of a suitable technology varies by societal characteristics and will change rapidly over time as new technologies (educational radio and television, computers, and various audio-visual instructional devices) become less expensive and more adaptable to a range of environments. The use of modern technology can also improve the management of basic education. Each country may reexamine periodically its present and potential technological capacity in relation to its basic educational needs and resources.

5 Mobilizing Information and Communication Channels

New possibilities are emerging which already show a powerful impact on meeting basic learning needs, and it is clear that the educational potential of these new possibilities has barely been tapped. These new possibilities exist largely as a result of two converging forces, both recent by-products of the general development process. First, the quantity of information available in the world - much of it relevant to survival and basic well-being - is exponentially greater than that available only a few years ago, and the rate of its growth is accelerating. A synergistic effect occurs when important information is coupled with a second modern advance - the new capacity to communicate among the people of the world. The opportunity exists to harness this force and use it positively, consciously, and with design, in order to contribute to meeting defined learning needs.

6 Building Partnerships and Mobilizing Resources

In designing the plan of action and creating a supportive policy environment for promoting basic education, maximum use of opportunities should be considered to expand existing collaborations and to bring together new partners: e.g., family and community organizations, non-governmental and other voluntary associations, teachers' unions, other professional groups, employers, the media, political parties, co-operatives, universities, research institutions, religious bodies, as well as education authorities and other government departments and services (labour, agriculture, health, information, commerce, industry, defence, etc.). The human and organizational resources these domestic partners represent need to be effectively mobilized to play their parts in implementing the plan of action. Partnerships at the community level and at the intermediate and national levels should be encouraged; they can help harmonize activities, utilize resources more effectively, and mobilize additional financial and human resources where necessary.

Governments and their partners can analyze the current allocation and use of financial and other resources for education and training in different sectors to determine if additional support for basic education can be obtained by

— improving efficiency,

— mobilizing additional sources of funding within and outside the government budget, and

— allocating funds within existing education and training budgets, taking into account efficiency and equity concerns. Countries where the total fiscal support for education is low need to explore the possibility of reallocating some public funds used for other purposes to basic education.

Assessing the resources actually or potentially available for basic education and comparing them to the budget estimates underlying the plan of action, can help identify possible inadequacies of resources that may affect the scheduling of planned activities over time or may require choices to be made. Countries that require external assistance to meet the basic learning needs of their people can use the resource assessment and plan of action as a basis for discussions with their international partners and for coordinating external funding.

The individual learners themselves constitute a vital human resource that needs to be mobilized. The demand for, and participation in, learning opportunities cannot simply be assumed, but must be actively encouraged. Potential learners need to see that the benefits of basic education activities exceed the costs the participants must bear, such as earnings foregone and reduced time available for community and household activities and for leisure. Women and girls especially may be deterred from taking full advantage of basic education opportunities because of reasons specific to individual cultures. Such barriers to participation may be overcome through the use of incentives and by programmes adapted to the local context and seen by the learners, their families and communities to be "productive activities". Also, learners tend to benefit more from education when they are partners in the instructional process, rather than treated simply as "inputs" or "beneficiaries". Attention to the issues of demand and participation will help assure that the learners' personal capacities are mobilized for education.

Family resources, including time and mutual support, are vital for the success of basic education activities. Families can be offered incentives and assistance to ensure that their resources are invested to enable all family members to benefit as fully and equitably as possible from basic education opportunities.

The preeminent role of teachers as well as of other educational personnel in providing quality basic education needs to be recognized and developed to optimize their contribution. This must entail measures to respect teachers' trade union rights and professional freedoms, and to improve their working conditions and status, notably in respect to their recruitment, initial and in-service training, remuneration and career development possibilities, as well as to allow teachers to fulfill their aspirations, social obligations, and ethical responsibilities.

In partnerships with school and community workers, libraries need to become a vital link in providing educational resources for all learners - pre-school through adulthood - in school and non-school settings. There is therefore a need to recognize libraries as invaluable information resources.

Community associations, co-operatives, religious bodies, and other non-governmental organizations also play important roles in supporting and in providing basic education. Their experience, expertise, energy and direct relationships with various constituencies are valuable resources for identifying and meeting basic learning needs. Their active involvement in partnerships for basic education should be promoted through policies and mechanisms that strengthen their capacities and recognize their autonomy.

2. Priority Action at Regional Level

Basic learning needs must be met through collaborative action within each country, but there are many forms of co-operation between countries with similar conditions and concerns that could, and do, assist in this endeavour. Regions have already developed plans, such as the Jakarta Plan of Action on Human Resources, adopted by ESCAP in 1988. By exchanging information and experience, pooling expertise, sharing facilities, and undertaking joint activities, several countries, working together, can increase their resource base and lower costs to their mutual benefit. Such arrangements are often set up among neighboring countries (sub-regional), among all countries in a major geo-cultural region, or among countries sharing a common language or having cultural and commercial relations. Regional and international organizations often play an important role in facilitating such co-operation between countries. In the following discussion, all such arrangements are included in the term "regional". In general, existing regional partnerships will need to be strengthened and provided with the resources necessary for their effective functioning in helping countries meet the basic learning needs of their populations.

1 Exchanging Information, Experience and Expertise

Various regional mechanisms, both intergovernmental and nongovernmental, promote co-operation in education and training, health, agricultural development, research and information, communications, and in other fields relevant to meeting basic learning needs. Such mechanisms can be further developed in response to the evolving needs of their constituents. Among several possible examples are the four regional programmes established through UNESCO in the 1980s to support national efforts to achieve universal primary education and eliminate adult illiteracy:

— Major Project in the Field of Education in Latin America and the Caribbean;

— Regional Programme for the Eradication of Illiteracy in Africa;

— Asia-Pacific Programme of Education for All (APPEAL);

— Regional Programme for the Universalization and Renewal of Primary Education and the Eradication of Illiteracy in the Arab States by the Year 2000 (ARABUPEAL).

In addition to the technical and policy consultations organized in connection with these programmes, other existing mechanisms can be used for consulting on policy issues in basic education. The conferences of ministers of education organized by UNESCO and by several regional organizations, the regular sessions of the regional commissions of the United Nations, and certain trans-regional conferences organized by the Commonwealth Secretariat, CONFEMEN (standing conference of ministers of education of francophone countries), the Organization of Economic Co-operation and Development (OECD), and the Islamic Educational, Scientific and Cultural Organization (ISESCO), could be used for this purpose as needs arise. In addition, numerous conferences and meetings organized by non-governmental bodies provide opportunities for professionals to share information and views on technical and policy issues. The conveners of these various conferences and meetings may consider ways of extending participation, where appropriate, to include representatives of other constituencies engaged in meeting basic learning needs. Full advantage should be taken of opportunities to share media messages or programmes that can be exchanged among countries or collaboratively developed, especially where language and cultural similarities extend beyond political boundaries.

2 *Undertaking Joint Activities*

There are many possible joint activities among countries in support of national efforts to implement action plans for basic education. Joint activities should be designed to exploit economies of scale and the comparative advantages of participating countries. Six areas where this form of regional collaboration seems particularly appropriate are:

— training of key personnel, such as planners, managers, teacher educators, researchers, etc. ;

— efforts to improve information collection and analysis;

— research;

— production of educational materials;

— use of communication media to meet basic learning needs; and

— management and use of distance education services.

Here, too, there are several existing mechanisms that could be utilized to foster such activities, including UNESCO's International Institute of Educational Planning and its networks of trainees and research as well as IBE's information network and the Unesco Institute for

Education, the five networks for educational innovation operating under UNESCO's auspices, the research and review advisory groups (RRAGs) associated with the International Development Research Centre, the Commonwealth of Learning, the Asian Cultural Center for UNESCO, the participatory network established by the International Council for Adult Education, and the International Association for the Evaluation of Educational Achievement, which links major national research institutions in some 35 countries. Certain multilateral and bilateral development agencies that have accumulated valuable experience in one or more of these areas might be interested in participating in joint activities. The five United Nations regional commissions could provide further support to such regional collaboration, especially by mobilizing policymakers to take appropriate action.

3. Priority Action at World Level

The world community has a well-established record of co-operation in education and development. However, international funding for education stagnated during the early 1980s; at the same time, many countries have been handicapped by growing debt burdens and economic relationships that channel their financial and human resources to wealthier countries. Because concern about the issues in basic education is shared by industrialized and developing countries alike, international co-operation can provide valuable support for national efforts and regional actions to implement the expanded vision of basic Education for All. Time, energy, and funding directed to basic education are perhaps the most profound investment in people and in the future of a country which can be made; there is a clear need and strong moral and economic argument for international solidarity to provide technical co-operation and financial assistance to countries that lack the resources to meet the basic learning needs of their populations.

1 Cooperation within the International Context

Meeting basic learning needs constitutes a common and universal human responsibility. The prospects for meeting basic learning needs around the world are determined in part by the dynamics of international relations and trade. With the current relaxation of tensions and the decreasing number of armed conflicts, there are now real possibilities to reduce the tremendous waste of military spending and shift those resources into socially useful areas, including basic education. The urgent task of meeting basic learning needs may require such a reallocation between sectors, and the world community and individual governments need to plan this conversion of resources for peaceful uses with courage and vision, and in a thoughtful and careful manner. Similarly, international measures to reduce or eliminate current imbalances in trade relations and to reduce debt burdens must be taken to enable many low-income countries to rebuild their own economies, releasing and retaining human and financial resources needed for development and for providing basic education to their populations. Structural adjustment policies should protect appropriate funding levels for education.

2 Enhancing National Capacities

International support should be provided, on request, to countries seeking to develop the national capacities needed for planning and managing basic education programmes and services. Ultimate responsibility rests within each nation to design and manage its own programmes to meet the learning needs of all its population. International support could include training and institutional development in data collection, analysis and research, technological innovation, and educational methodologies. Management information systems and other modern management methods could also be introduced, with an emphasis on low and middle level managers. These capabilities will be even more in demand to support quality improvements in primary education and to introduce innovative out-of-school programmes. In addition to direct support to countries and institutions, international assistance can also be usefully channelled to support the activities of international, regional and other inter-country structures that organize joint research, training and information exchanges. The latter should be based on, and supported by, existing institutions and programmes, if need be improved and strengthened, rather than on the establishment of new structures. Support will be especially valuable for technical cooperation among developing countries, among whom both circumstances and resources available to respond to circumstances are often similar.

3 Providing Sustained Long-term Support for National and Regional Actions

Meeting the basic learning needs of all people in all countries is obviously a long-term undertaking. This Framework provides guidelines for preparing national and subnational plans of action for the development of basic education through a long-term commitment of governments and their national partners to work together to reach the targets and achieve the objectives they set for themselves. International agencies and institutions, many of which are sponsors, co-sponsors, and associate sponsors of the World Conference on Education for All, should actively seek to plan together and sustain their long-term support for the kinds of national and regional actions outlined in the preceding sections. In particular, the core sponsors of the Education for All initiative (UNDP, UNESCO, UNICEF, World Bank) affirm their commitments to supporting the priority areas for international action presented below and to making appropriate arrangements for meeting the objectives of Education for All, each acting within its mandate, special responsibilities, and decisions of its governing bodies. Given that UNESCO is the UN agency with a particular responsibility for education, it will give priority to implementing the Framework for Action and to facilitating provision of services needed for reinforced international co-ordination and co-operation.

Increased international funding is needed to help the less developed countries implement their own autonomous plans of action in line with the expanded vision of basic Education for All. Genuine partnerships characterized by co-operation and joint long-term commitments will accomplish more and provide the basis for a substantial increase in overall funding for this important sub-sector of education. Upon governments' request, multilateral and bilateral agencies should focus on supporting priority actions, particularly at the country level, in areas such as the following:

1. The design or updating of national and subnational multisectoral plans of action, which will need to be

elaborated very early in the 1990s. Both financial and technical assistance are needed by many developing countries, particularly in collecting and analyzing data, as well as in organizing domestic consultations.

2. National efforts and related inter-country co-operation to attain a satisfactory level of quality and relevance in primary education. Experiences involving the participation of families, local communities, and non-governmental organizations in increasing the relevance and improving the quality of education could profitably be shared among countries.

3. The provision of universal primary education in the economically poorer countries. International funding agencies should consider negotiating arrangements to provide long-term support, on a case-by-case basis, to help countries move toward universal primary education according to their timetable. The external agencies should examine current assistance practices in order to find ways of effectively assisting basic education programmes which do not require capital- and technology-intensive assistance, but often need longer-term budgetary support. In this context, greater attention should be given to criteria for development co-operation in education to include more than mere economic considerations.

4. Programmes designed to meet the basic learning needs of disadvantaged groups, out-of-school youth, and adults with little or no access to basic learning opportunities. All partners can share their experience and expertise in designing and implementing innovative measures and activities, and focus their funding for basic education on specific categories and

groups (e.g., women, the rural poor, the disabled) to improve significantly the learning opportunities and conditions available for them.

5. Education programmes for women and girls. These programmes should be designed to eliminate the social and cultural barriers which have discouraged or even excluded women and girls from benefits of regular education programmes, as well as to promote equal opportunities in all aspects of their lives.

6. Education programmes for refugees. The programmes run by such organizations as the United Nations High Commission for Refugees (UNHCR) and the United Nations Relief and Works Agency for Palestine (UNRWA) need more substantial and reliable long-term financial support for this recognized international responsibility. Where countries of refuge need international financial and technical assistance to cope with the basic needs of refugees, including their learning needs, the international community can help to share this burden through increased cooperation. The world community will also endeavour to ensure that people under occupation or displaced by war and other calamities continue to have access to basic education programmes that preserve their cultural identity.

7. Basic education programmes of all kinds in countries with high rates of illiteracy (as in sub-Saharan Africa) and with large illiterate populations (as in South Asia). Substantial assistance will be needed to reduce significantly the world's large number of illiterate adults.

8. Capacity building for research and planning and the experimentation of small-scale innovations. The

success of Education for All actions will ultimately be determined by the capacity of each country to design and implement programs that reflect national conditions. A strengthened knowledge base nourished by research findings and the lessons of experiments and innovations as well as the availablity of competent educational planners will be essential in this respect.

The coordination of external funding for education is an area of shared responsibility at country level, in which host governments need to take the lead to ensure the efficient use of resources in accordance with their priorities. Development funding agencies should explore innovative and more flexible modalities of co-operation in consultation with the governments and institutions with which they work and co-operate in regional initiatives, such as the Task Force of Donors to African Education. Other forums need to be developed in which funding agencies and developing countries can collaborate in the design of inter-country projects and discuss general issues relating to financial assistance.

4 Consultations on Policy Issues

Existing channels of communication and forums for consultation among the many partners involved in meeting basic learning needs should be fully utilized in the 1990s to maintain and extend the international consensus underlying this Framework for Action. Some channels and forums, such as the biannual International Conference on Education, operate globally, while others focus on particular regions or groups of countries or categories of partners. Insofar as possible, organizers should seek to coordinate these consultations and share results. Moreover, in order to maintain and expand the Education for All initiative, the international community will need to make appropriate arrangements, which will ensure co-operation among the interested agencies using the existing mechanisms insofar as possible:

— to continue advocacy of basic Education for All, building on the momentum generated by the World Conference;

— to facilitate sharing information on the progress made in achieving basic education targets set by countries for themselves and on the resources and organizational requirements for successful initiatives;

— to encourage new partners to join this global endeavor; and

— to ensure that all partners are fully aware of the importance of maintaining strong support for basic education.

Indicative Phasing of Implementation for the 1990s

Each country, in determining its own intermediate goals and targets and in designing its plan of action for achieving them, will, in the process, establish a timetable to harmonize and schedule specific activities. Similarly, regional and international action will need to be scheduled to help countries meet their targets on time. The following general schedule suggests an indicative phasing during the 1990s; of course, certain phases may need to overlap and the dates indicated will need to be adapted to individual country and organizational contexts.

Governments and organizations set specific targets and complete or update their plans of action to meet basic learning needs take measures to create a supportive policy environment; devise policies to improve the relevance, quality, equity and efficiency of basic education services and programmes; design the means to adapt information and communication media to meet basic learning needs and mobilize resources and establish operational partnership. International partners assist countries, through direct support and through regional co-operation, to complete this preparatory stage.

Development agencies establish policies and plans for the 1990s, in line with their commitments to sustained, long-term support for national and regional actions and increase their financial and technical assistance to basic education accordingly (III.3). All partners strengthen and use relevant existing mechanisms for consultation and co-operation and establish procedures for monitoring progress at regional and international levels.

First stage of implementation of plans of action: national coordinating bodies monitor implementation and propose appropriate adjustments to plans. Regional and international supporting actions are carried out.

Governments and organizations undertake mid-term evaluation of the implementation of their respective plans and adjust them as needed. Governments, organizations and development agencies undertake comprehensive policy reviews at regional and global levels.

Second stage of implementation of plans of action and of supporting action at regional and international levels. Development agencies adjust their plans as necessary and increase their assistance to basic education accordingly.

Governments, organizations and development agencies evaluate achievements and undertake comprehensive policy review at regional and global levels.

There will never be a better time to renew commitment to the inevitable and long-term effort to meet the basic learning needs of all children, youth and adults. This effort will require a much greater and wiser investment of resources in basic education and training than ever before, but benefits will begin accruing immediately and will extend well into the future — where the global challenges of today will be met, in good measure, by the world community's commitment and perseverance in attaining its goal of education for all.

2

Global Initiatives on Education

The World Education Forum reaffirmed the vision of the World Declaration on Education for All (EFA) that all children, young people and adults have the human right to benefit from an education that will meet their basic learning needs in the best and fullest sense of the term. The Forum collectively committed itself to attaining the following goals:

(i) expanding and improving comprehensive early childhood care and education, especially for the most vulnerable and disadvantaged children.

(ii) ensuring that by 2015 all children, particularly girls, children in difficult circumstances and those belonging to ethnic minorities, have access to and complete, free and compulsory primary education of good quality.

(iii) ensuring that the learning needs of all young people and adults are met through equitable access to appropriate learning and life-skills programmes.

(iv) achieving a 50 per cent improvement in levels of adult literacy by 2015, especially for women, and equitable access to basic and continuing education for all adults.

(v) eliminating gender disparities in primary and secondary education by 2005, and achieving gender equality in education by 2015, with a focus on ensuring girls' full and equal access to and achievement in basic education of good quality.

(vi) improving all aspects of the quality of education and ensuring excellence of all so that recognized and measurable learning outcomes are achieved by all, especially in literacy, numeracy and essential life skills.

2. In addition to the six goals, the Forum identified a number of particularly critical themes, for example HIV/AIDS, teachers and quality of education, education in situations of emergency and crisis, and Information Technology (IT), as needing immediate attention and action.

The EFA goals underline the long-existing and prevailing concerns of the international community that have been expressed in numerous declarations and conventions since the Universal Declaration of Human Rights in 1948 stipulated free education for all - a goal reaffirmed in the Convention on the Rights of the Child in 1989. Two of the EFA goals, universal primary education by 2015 and elimination of gender disparity in primary and secondary education by 2005, also form part of the recognized international development targets that aim at global poverty reduction through strategies for health and the environment in addition to those for education. Proposed at the World Summit for Social Development in Copenhagen in 1995, these targets were agreed by the Development Assistance Committee (DAC) of the

Organisation for Economic Co-operation and Development (OECD) in 1996. They were reaffirmed in the United Nations Millennium Declaration in 2000.

The EFA goals highlight the downside of globalization, namely marginalization and exclusion of certain population groups, countries and regions that have persisted, even grown more extensive, despite the numerous international declarations and conventions issued since the Second World War in support of free education for all, equity, social development and poverty reduction.

According to the Dakar Framework, more than 113 million children have no access to primary education, 880 million adults are illiterate, gender discrimination continues to permeate education systems, and the quality of learning and acquisition of human values and skills fall far short of the aspirations and needs of individuals and societies.

Furthermore, disruptive conditions related to, for example, persistent civil wars and the HIV/AIDS pandemic, call for radical rethinking of, or at least a much wider range of approaches to, the teaching and learning process. They also highlight the relevance of the Dakar focus themes and the need to find diversified solutions for countries in different circumstances, including those in emergency, crisis or post-conflict situations.

The plea of the late 1980s for structural adjustment with a human face or the need to protect the vulnerable while promoting growth thus continues to be valid. Furthermore, there continues to be a strong contrast between official government support for the international declarations and their implementation, despite relative consistency in the thinking on the necessity and benefits of education for development. Investment in human and social capital are now widely accepted as means of creating sustainable development, achieving poverty reduction and reducing inequalities within and among nations, and of enhancing personal development and quality of life.

The synergy between education and improved health, higher productivity, innovation, increased political participation and empowerment is comparatively well established, although many of the precise mechanisms still have to be more clearly understood because of differences in outcomes in different contexts. Significantly, education is the critical force in creating tolerance, respect for diversity and peaceful understanding - a purpose which has gained even more significance in light of recent developments on the world scene.

Education is also central to the current, pervasive emphasis to establish a mutually reinforcing relationship between macro-economic stability and structural reform on one hand, and growth and reduction of poverty and inequality on the other. This is reflected in the outcomes of top-level meetings, such as those of the G8 countries in Cologne in 1999 and in Genoa in 2001 and of the G7 education ministers in Tokyo in 2000 at which investment in lifelong learning, education and skills was placed at the core of the development of future information-based societies. "Education and skills are indispensable to achieving economic success, civic responsibility and social cohesion", as stated in the 1999 Cologne charter. The G8 leaders in Okinawa agreed, according to their communique:

> to follow up vigorously the conclusions of the recent Dakar conference on Education for All by ensuring that additional resources are made available for basic education.... [And, in accordance with the Dakar Framework for Action] reaffirm our commitment that no government seriously committed to achieving Education for All will be thwarted in this achievement by lack of resources. ... [Moreover] ... to strengthen efforts bilaterally and together with international organizations and private sector donors to achieve the goals of universal primary education by 2015 and gender equality in schooling by 2005.

The leaders in Okinawa also called on international financial institutions, in partnership with developing countries, to focus on education in their poverty reduction strategies and to provide greater assistance for countries with sound education strategies. "These strategies should maximise the potential benefits of IT in this area through distance learning wherever possible and other effective means," the leaders stressed. This theme was underlined again at the Genoa meeting in 2001 when the G8 countries also reaffirmed their "commitment to help countries meet the Dakar Framework for Action goal of universal primary education by 2015".

Thus, while education's central role in development efforts is undisputed and backed by high-level political commitment in the case of Education for All, not all EFA goals seem to carry the same weight. The wider development targets and millennium goals supported by the statements of the G8 countries do not address the expanded basic education concept of the World Declaration on Education for All (World Conference on Education for All, 1990) and the focus of the Dakar Framework for Action. In particular, the development targets for universal primary education and gender equality neglect the strong emphasis of the Dakar goals on the quality of education. It is essential that attention be paid to the expanded concept of basic education and to all six Dakar goals. These must be interpreted comprehensively in the context of support for intermediary and higher-level education in order to achieve holistic development processes.

The Global Campaign for Education is now emphasizing the importance of the initiative as a ledger and mechanism to monitor fulfilment of commitments both by national governments and by development partners related to such aspects as the formulation and implementation of EFA plans, identification of resource gaps, and brokering and channelling of financing. The World Bank (and UNDP) have also, in accordance with the Dakar Framework for Action, linked the global initiative to the fulfilment of the commitment to fund viable national EFA plans in the context of an overall poverty reduction framework, specifically the World Bank Poverty Reduction Strategy Papers (PRSP), the Enhanced Heavily Indebted Poor Countries (HIPC) Initiative and the Comprehensive Development Framework (CDF).

According to the Bank (and UNDP), implementing the initiative would require massive partnerships based on a division of labour and identification of tasks in light of the comparative advantage of all partners. In the view of the Bank (and UNDP), this should rest on a three-pronged strategy aiming at:

(1) reaching consensus on policy and technical issues recognized as barriers to development of basic education, especially in HIPC;

(2) undertaking key non-lending activities to help countries identify gaps, financial or others, hindering the achievement of EFA; and

(3) developing an implementation strategy aimed at increasing the effectiveness of international assistance.

The World Bank is currently examining the practical implications of establishing a global financial mechanism for EFA.

According to these suggestions, the nature of the global initiative is rather understood as a mechanism for short-term support, in particular to strengthen incentives for governments to prepare and implement plans, and for comprehensive policy dialogue. According to the Bank, particular attention should be paid to reaching consensus on the definition of a national plan, criteria for countries to join the initiative, mobilization of extra financial resources and ensuring regular, transparent monitoring of subsequent policy dialogue and action.

This focus can be regarded as justifiable in light of the first, time-bound goal in the Dakar Framework for Action, namely that countries must produce national EFA action plans by 2002, either through modification of existing national education plans in accordance with the Dakar goals or through development of new ones. This would, however, limit the wider development perspectives that support for education and the Dakar goals are intended to serve and restrict the understanding of resources which are here understood as financial, human, material and non-material in nature. Finally, while deployment of resources must be strategically targeted, the principle for the global initiative, as interpreted here, is to assist in creating the preconditions necessary for as many countries as possible to join it and to apply the initiative in accordance with diversified needs.

There are ongoing efforts in the World Bank, UNESCO and other organizations to estimate the financial resources needed to achieve Education for All. They include attempts both at establishing a global financing goal and at identifying resource gaps at the country level. In line with the international development targets, current calculations have focused on estimating the financial resource gap to meet the goal of universal primary education by 2015 which has been interpreted based on either gross (in the case of the World Bank) or net (in the case of UNESCO) enrolment figures. Because of the difficulty of measuring qualitative aspects of universal primary education and of the lack of focus on the other five EFA goals, the indicative figures remain questionable, highlighting the difficulty of the concept of a global funding gap.

According to the World Bank, current funding for education budgets in developing countries originates predominantly from national governments (97 per cent) while the international community provides only 3 per cent of the total, of which 1.5 per cent represents World Bank funding. Other calculations indicate that up to 10 per cent of total funding comes from the international community. This proportion can be even higher (by some estimated at 40 per cent) in specific countries. In general, funding from the international community is considered to play a critical, catalytic and supportive role.

Set in the context of education's critical multi-purpose role in societal and personal development, the relative proportion of total education funding in developing countries provided by the international community is small. The highest figure estimated to reach UPE by 2015 ($15 billion in addition to what is currently spent) represents less than 0.3 per cent of the total GNP of the developing countries, 0.06 per cent of the total GNP of developed countries and 0.05 per cent of the world's GNP. While enhanced national resource mobilization, utilization and management is critical, the international community must comply with its stated commitment to concerted action that will lead to increased support for national EFA efforts along the lines of the Dakar Framework for Action. Such efforts are particularly important in light of recent international developments. They must be well integrated with other international efforts to reduce poverty and global, regional and national inequalities.

The six elements for resource mobilization and efficiency measures identified for the global initiative in the Dakar Framework (increasing external finance; greater predictability in the flow of external assistance; earlier, more extensive and broader debt relief; effective donor coordination; sector-wide approaches; and monitoring) must be understood and applied as a function of the different institutional and structural contexts and constraints at the national level that would determine the specific approaches and strategies adopted by development partners and national governments. In this respect, macro-economic and sectoral reform must be linked in order to ensure a supportive environment that would enable the education system to function efficiently and effectively as a development tool. Reform efforts must include policy reform to enhance locally generated resources for education and other development purposes through, for example, more effective fiscal instruments, appropriate taxation and taxation incentives, enhanced private sector contributions and budgetary re-allocations, and the attraction of additional private international capital flows, concessional resources and improved measures for debt relief. All resources and expenditures must be treated within a common budgetary framework. Simultaneous policy reform of the education sector must aim at cost-shifting and cost-sharing.

Cost-sharing should be undertaken without adverse effects for the poor and without enhancing gender, rural/urban, regional and other inequalities, thus implying at the same time the elimination of direct and indirect user fees at the basic level. The efficiency and effectiveness of the teaching-learning processes must be heightened through locally adapted solutions, including the use of new information technologies. This also includes the adoption of sector-wide approaches to educational development and improving aid conditionalities.

Support for EFA must form part of other education sector support and of the core elements of a government's budget. EFA must be linked within sector frameworks with poverty reduction and development strategies. This means coherence among national Education for All action plans, education sector plans, development strategies and other policy frameworks, such as the Common Country Assessments (CCA), the United Nations Development Assistance Framework (UNDAF), CDF, PRSPs and the HIPC Initiative.

International and national resource mobilization must, thus, be complementary and well targeted in pursuit of holistic national development processes. Such mobilization depends on high-level political commitment of both national governments and international agencies. Global and national redistribution of resources through, for example, improved trade conditions or budgetary re-allocations might be particularly instrumental in filling the estimated funding gap both in the short and the long term.

In the current context of increased international security measures, it will be particularly important not only to protect education and wider social sector spending, but to invest at a level that can guarantee their critical functions for poverty reduction, sustainable development and international peace and solidarity. Further development and implementation of the global initiative must, therefore, continue to involve all EFA partners and must form part of the thinking on financing and development in organizations, such as the Bretton Woods institutions, OECD and the G8.

The need for innovative thinking in resource mobilization is partly related to the discouraging trend in Official Development Assistance (ODA) and other financial flows during the 1990s. Total net resource flows to aid recipient countries of which ODA forms a part, more than doubled during 1991-96 (from $138 billion to $354 billion), but declined severely during 1996-98 because of the Asian financial crisis and have only somewhat recovered in recent years. The proportional share of Official Development Finance (ODF) (which includes ODA) dropped from two-thirds to one third of the total during 1991-99, private flows having gained comparative importance with a peak of 78% of the total in 1996 when ODF was at its lowest.

As a percentage of the combined GNP of OECD/DAC member countries, ODA has fallen by more than one-fifth in constant dollar terms, from 0.33% in 1992 to its lowest level of 0.22% in 1997 with some slight recovery to 0.24% in 1999. Real net ODA disbursements (in constant 1998 prices) fell from $60,421 million in 1992 to $48,324 million in 1997, then increased to $55,343 in 1999.

Four member countries (Denmark, the Netherlands, Norway and Sweden) were joined in 2000 by Luxemburg, according to provisional figures, in having fulfilled the United Nations target of allocating 0.7 per cent or more of GNP for international development assistance.

The largest four economies, France, Germany, Japan and United States, together with Canada and Italy, have had the greatest reductions in their assistance during the 1990s, although the trend for Japan has been positive since 1998 because of special contributions in light of the Asian financial crisis. By contrast, the non-G7 group have allocated increased shares throughout the 1990s and additional, smaller countries have joined in this support.

Aid allocations have declined in all regions except for Europe and Central Asia, and East Asia and the Pacific during the 1990s. The trend for the least developed countries has been downward in recent years, sub-Saharan Africa having witnessed the sharpest decline, by roughly one-third. Some of the major aid providers are responsible for some of the largest reductions.

The ODA proportion of total net resource flows was halved during 1991-98 (from 41.4% to an estimated 20.7%) with respect to both bilateral and multilateral funds. Of total multilateral real net disbursements, non-concessional funding gained importance over concessional funding during the 1990s. EC and the International Development Association (IDA) provided roughly one-third of concessional real flows in 1999, with the Inter-American Development Bank (IDB), IBRD and the Asian Development Bank (ADB) being the main providers of non-concessional real flows.

It is noteworthy that education seems to have suffered relatively less within this overall declining ODA trend. This must be judged, however, against rather low allocations in individual countries' overall development assistance for education, generally, and for basic education, specifically. Of total DAC bilateral allocations, education seems to have maintained its proportional share constituting roughly 11% in both 1989 and 1999, whereas multilateral allocations increased from 4.6 to 7.6% in the same years.

The absolute value of bilateral commitments to education was largely unchanged in 1999 compared to 1990 (roughly $3,980 million in constant 1998 prices), having experienced a high of $4,341 million in 1994. Multilateral funding increased by only roughly $300 million during 1990-97. Bilateral support for basic education amounted to only $703 million, on average, in 1997-98, constituting 1.2% of total bilateral ODA commitments. Of multilateral financial commitments (ODF), basic education constituted 4.8% in 1999.

The EFA partners are, therefore, faced with several challenges.

First, they should radically increase support for basic education and for overall international development assistance. This has become even more crucial in the currently difficult international security situation. Increased financing must be ccompanied by greater predictability in the flow of external assistance and maximum reliance on all available and possible new funding sources, including debt relief and/or debt cancellation for basic education.

Second, they must ensure that increased financial flows, ODA as well as private financing, act as a catalyst for national resource mobilization and sustainable development with due attention to the critical role of basic education. This would require targeting of resources and setting conditionalities in view of differential needs in specific regions and countries.

Third, they should strengthen policy coherence and coordination of EFA efforts nationally and internationally, adopt sector-wide approaches and strengthen partnerships with all EFA actors. This will ensure that the various international initiatives related to the international development targets promote the Dakar EFA goals and basic education.

Fourth, they must hold national governments and the international community to their commitment to EFA through careful monitoring of the progress towards the EFA goals and targets. This will include monitoring of financing for (basic) education as well as identification of constraints and opportunities for planning, formulation and implementation of national EFA goals and targets.

RESOLUTIONS ADOPTED BY 3RD WORLD CONGRESS OF EDUCATION INTERNATIONAL MEETING IN JOMEITIN IN 2001

Educating in a Global Economy

Preamble

1. Education is the key to participation in the global economy of the 21st century, based on technological revolutions in communications and transfer of information, as well as major changes in production,

transport and distribution, and the economic value of knowledge. This global economy is based upon levels of mobility unprecedented in human history—mobility of information, of finance, of goods and services, and of people, but also mobility of disease, of crime, of arms and instruments of repression. Extremes of wealth and poverty within and among countries are greater than ever. In this new era with its opportunities and threats, each of the principal aims of Education International is more relevant than ever in seeking to build societies that are fair and just for all their citizens, that respect universal values of democracy and human rights, and whose development—social as well as economic—will be equitable and sustainable. In every country, this global economy seeks to permanently reduce the labour cost, and questions the right to education, and to qualification.

The development of quality higher education systems in developing countries (alongside the expansion of primary, secondary and vocational education) is an essential precondition for the training of the specialists needed for economic and social development, as well as for capacity-building within the education sector as a whole;

2. Education has always reflected and been influenced by changes in economy and society, while at the same time acting upon those changes. The relationship between education, economy and society is interactive. At a time of rapid and even fundamental changes in economy and society, there are great new challenges for education:

— achieving Education for All;

— making life-long learning a reality for all;

— reaffirming the values of education in relation to personal development, the world of work and the rights and responsibilities of citizenship in demo-cratic societies;

— rethinking educational content and methods, taking into account the potential and the consequences of new technologies;

— recruiting enough qualified people to work in the education sector;

— defining the key role of the teacher as a specialist in the provision and management of learning opportunities;

— interacting with a broader spectrum of partners, parents and local communities, trade unions and enterprises, and non-governmental organisations;

3. There are also threats to education arising out of the global economy:

— commercialisation of educational services, with consequent risks of inequity, discrimination and deepening of the digital divide;

— non-respect for diversity of culture, traditions and languages;

— introduction, under the guise of 'reform', of a 'culture of enterprise' based on self-interest, with the consequent risk of undermining the ethical values of education and of the teaching profession;

— decreasing attention to the values underlying democracy, and increasing attention to the values of competition and the market;

— short-sighted solutions to the new challenges, such as hiring unqualified people or draining teachers from the south towards the north;

— changes in the role of the State, with more emphasis on regulation and less on guarantees of equity and non-discrimination;

4. Huge public funds are being released to encourage the development of on-line education, and the promise of an education via new technologies is being used as an excuse to deny legitimate claims regarding the building or the upgrading of schools and the recruitment of new teachers and personnel of all categories.

   More and more students are deprived of their right to study, as they are compelled to follow electronic courses and watch video-conferences instead of following regular courses. University institutions are trying to seize teachers' intellectual property rights and plan to sell their courses to other universities, to business and to indivi-dual buyers. This leads to the privatisation of schools and to the emergence of specialised firms;

The Third World Congress of Education International, meeting in Jomtien, Thailand, from 25 to 29 July, 2001:

Calls on all Governments:

— *to draw up* national action plans by December 2002 for Education For All, using transparent and democratic processes based on the development and improvement of a public education service, involving the various partners, particularly education unions, parents, students and NGOs active in the education sector;

— *ratify and implement* the ILO Convention adopted in June 1999 forbidding the worst forms of child labour, for the purpose of bringing a definitive end to all forms of exploitation of children;

— *endeavour* to concretely implement the decisions of the Jomtien and Dakar conferences on Education For All;

— *to establish* consultative processes with partners in educational reform;

— *to take steps*, in close consultation with education unions, for the recruitment of sufficient qualified teachers and other educational personnel;

— *to enter* into negotiations with education unions in order to upgrade the status of the teaching profession;

— *to take* the necessary political decisions to ensure adequate funding of education at all levels, with a minimum allocation of 6 percent of Gross National Product (GNP);

— *to establish* a tax on financial transactions (Tobin tax) in order to fight against financial speculation and instability while finding new funds for the education systems in developing countries;

Calls on member countries of the OECD:

— *to implement* the proposals of the G8 Summits and complete them in order to obtain the writing off of the debt of the least developed countries, on the understanding that resources so saved will be re-allocated by those countries to education and health;

— *to raise* levels of official development assistance to 0.7 percent of GNP, and to give priority to assistance in achieving the goals of the education for all campaign, as well as basic health measures for all families;

— *to give* special attention to cooperative teacher education programs in developing countries, and to respect the interests of those countries when recruiting teachers;

Calls on the United Nations, its specialised agencies and programs, and other intergovernmental agencies:

— *to coordinate* their efforts towards achievement of the goals of the Declaration of Dakar - Education For All before the year 2015;

— *to take* advantage of the World Summit on Sustainable Development (Rio + 10, Johannesburg 2002) to emphasise basic education as the main tool for confronting worldwide problems such as environmental degra-dation, demographic growth and "consumerist" waste;

— *to act* in order to take, as quickly as possible, within the Kyoto protocol framework, concrete and constraining measures submitted to effective monitoring mechanisms;

— *to mobilise* the efforts of the international community so as to raise the resources necessary for the attainment of these goals;

— *to respect*, throughout the UN systems and other intergovernmental agencies, the ILO Declaration on Fundamental Principles and Rights at Work;

— *to work* with the trade union movement, business and organisations of civil society on issues arising from the erosion of national tax bases and new approaches to financing global needs in a global economy;

— *to give* priority to balanced investment in all levels of education without resort to redistribution of funds from one educational sector to another;

Congress recommends that EI *and its member organisations*:

— *maintain* the campaign for quality public education for all, in cooperation with its non-governmental and inter-governmental partners, and the campaign against child labour;

— *take* all the initiatives at the national, regional and international levels to defend and improve the public education system, thereby guaranteeing the pedagogical freedom of the teacher according to the 1966 UNESCO/ILO Recommendation and the rights of the young and adults to a basic and lifelong quality education, and that they be interlocutors recognised by the political leadership in the field of education;

— *advocate* through interventions to intergovernmental agencies and national governments, and campaigns directed at public opinion, a concept of education based on quality provision for all by qualified and motivated educators, and the personal development of free men and women able to contribute to society, not merely units of production;

— *oppose* in principle the commodification of education and research services by the WTO and the General Agreement on Trade in Services (GATS) and monitor closely any moves to apply the GATS to education and research services and mobilise against such moves in appropriate ways, including campaigns directed at public opinion;

— *give* particular attention to the issue of teacher recruitment and related issues of the status of the teaching profession;

— *share* research and information on conditions and trends in education and teaching;

— *undertake* an analysis of the impact of the global economy on copyright and related issues of intellectual property affecting teachers, as well as standards of educational materials, including educational software, and respect for cultural diversity;

— *promote* continuing solidarity among the member organi-sations of Education International, through development and emergency assistance, mobilisation against violations of human and trade union rights, and the extension of information and communication technology;

— *give* high priority to enhancing the activism of member organisations to enable them to respond to the threats to public education posed by neo-liberal economic and education policies being pursued by global institutions such as the World Bank, IMF and WTO. New programs are urgently needed for development with human and labour rights and the public provision of high quality community services such as education.

— *develop* the key role which EI can play in assisting member organisations to campaign more effectively through activities which educate and mobilise members and which support them in building alliances with NGOs and other community movements which share the objectives of EI;

— *focus* attention on the key demand to exclude education and other basic social services from agreements which national governments may reach in the framework of the General Agreement on Trade in Services (GATS), or bilateral and regional trade agreements.

Partnership to achieve education for all

The Third World Congress of Education International, meeting in Jomtien, Thailand, from 25 to 29 July, 2001:

Notes that:

1. Over 115 million primary-school-age children do not attend school and large numbers of children drop out before they have reached grade 5;
2. Of the 882 million illiterates in the world, 63.7 per cent are women;
3. More than two thirds of the governments in the world allocate less than the minimum of 6 per cent of their Gross National Product (GNP) to education as recommended by the Delors Commission;
4. The majority of industrialised countries do not allocate 0.7 per cent of their GNP to development as recommended by the UN General Assembly, and only a small part of the funds provided for development is allocated to basic education;
5. The ambitions and objectives determined by world organizations and forums are constantly revised down-wards, and they are not respected;

Believes that:

6. All governments have a responsibility to fulfil their human rights obligation to provide, free and compulsory basic education of good quality for all children, especially girls, youth, immigrants, indigenous students, children with special needs or in difficult circumstances and those belonging to ethnic minorities, in accordance with the commitment made in the Dakar Framework for Action by 2015. In today's world, the mission of quality public schooling is not limited to the basic years of education, but includes secondary school and the acquisition of vocational qualifications;
7. It is not sufficient to improve enrolment figures without considering the quality of education;
8. Partnership is a key concept for the achievement of education for all. The objective of the different parties must be the common interest. Proposals and activities must be implemented respecting the responsibilities of the different partners, and financing must preserve the public character of education;

Recommends that:

9. Teacher trade unions approach ministries of education and form partnerships where possible, with the shared objective of achieving education for all;
10. The ministries put in place a mechanism for information, consultations and negotiations aimed at improving teachers' salaries and working conditions, the resources, learning materials and equipment in schools, teacher education and the training of educational personnel;

11. Teacher unions take initiatives which will support improvements in the quality of education;
12. Schools be based on democratic participation, and accountability to civil society, a partnership to elaborate new ways of co-operation between school and parents, a partnership between schools, and trade unions and different sectors of the community, and a shared commitment to combat child labour;
13. Without putting into question the priority role of public formal education, new forms of cooperation and broad national alliances be sought, particularly with NGOs, in order to develop complementary forms of education in the context of the objectives of education for all;
14. A universal commitment to education for all must include reforms of International Monetary Fund and World Bank structural adjustment policies; a programme for debt cancellation; increased allocations to free public education at all levels in the development co-operation budgets of the industrialised countries; and further examination of the possibilities for developing international agreements on investment, financial transactions and taxation that will prevent situations where countries are not able to levy or collect the taxes needed to improve education systems;
15. Teacher unions, other unions and trade union centres form alliances around shared objectives to achieve education for all;

EI *should*:

16. Prepare a detailed plan of action as part of the Global Campaign for Education in co-operation with other

organisations, to pressure governments to meet their obligation to provide free public quality education for all.

Education and New Technology

The Third World Congress of Education International, meeting in Jomtien, Thailand, from 25 to 29 July, 2001:

1. *Considers* that the use of new information and communication technologies (ICT) in education and training will develop further, as is already the case in most other professional sectors;

2. *Considers* that their use may create opportunities for more widespread and diversified access to knowledge, but will pose at the same time major challenges for education personnel and their unions. ICT must be the means of improving education and strenghthening union rights by facilitating access to information, and democracy;

3. *Notes* that currently, the use of new information and communication technologies (ICT) in traditional systems of education and training, or outside these systems, generates inequality in terms of access, not only between industrialised and developing countries, but also between the privileged and the disadvantaged in all countries;

4. *Stresses* that it is in the nature of the trade union movement to take these challenges into consideration and to define appropriate strategies so that new information and communication technologies (ICT) become an instrument of democratisation providing access to "quality public education for all". Teachers

must keep the key role in the learning processwhich will consist in knowledge and education for citizenship. This new learning needs a development of research in education to explore and analyse the different pedagogical ways of using ICT. Teachers must be associated with this research so they can take advantage of its results;

5. *Stresses* that the virtual marketing and export of education, particularly at the level of higher education, has resulted in the opening of a huge market to ambitious investors taking advantage of the current political and economic environment;

6. *Stresses* that the huge financial stakes inherent in the commercialisation of knowledge pose a problem of intellectual property rights and of the qualitative design, production and dissemination of software, along with the risk of the existence of e-learning monopolies to the detriment of the cultural diversity, conservation of ethnic identity, values and history of our societies;

7. *Stresses* that the increasingly substantial and diversified supply of courses on the Internet raises the question of their quality and of the accreditation of diplomas obtained by those who follow these courses;

8. *Stresses* that effective digital learning will require more teachers with higher skills than ever before with subsequent implications for the provision of training and support;

9. *Stresses* that public education must play its part to give teachers professional tools (producing and circulating software) inspired by true educational and pedagogical choices.

The Third World Congress of Education International:

10. *Demands* that all teachers and education personnel receive adequate training in the use of new information and communication technologies (ICT) and that gradually all schools be connected to the Internet free of charge, with the necessary access restrictions and security protocols (filters, firewall, etc.) to guarantee strictly pedagogical usage.The collective dimension through ICT and the role of team work of teachers must be taken in account in this training;
11. *Mandates* the Executive Board to carry on the necessary discussions with UNESCO, other relevant bodies, the OECD and governments to ensure that the design, production and dissemination of education software will be organised appropriately to guarantee the cultural diversity, conservation of ethnic identity, values and history required for international understanding;
12. *Mandates* the Executive Board to carry on the necessary discussions with UNESCO, other relevant bodies, the OECD and governments so that education will not be considered as a commodity, and intergovernmental cultural agreements and principles of UNESCO will prevail over the commercial rules of WTO in the exchanges of education services;
13. *Mandates* the Executive Board to vigorously advocate the provisions and use of learning software and to pursue means of providing software at prices affordable to developing countries, and to encourage a better distribution of knowledge to all;

14. *Mandates* the Executive Board to defend the interests of education personnel with respect to working conditions, career opportunities and intellectual property rights and to develop codes of good practice on these and related issues;

15. *Mandates* the Executive Board to take the necessary action to determine the impact of technology, in particular the potential hazards to children's health and safety but also its effects on young children's learning environment;

16. *Mandates* EI and member organisations to support national and international research into the educational, social and economic impacts of technological developments affecting education and the working conditions of teachers;

17. *Mandates* the Executive Board to undertake the necessary action so that public authorities can take advantage of the technological revolution to guarantee the fair distribution of information and knowledge, and to carry on the necessary consciousness-raising activities with civil society organisations on the great opportunities presented by this revolution but also on the challenges it poses to "quality public education for all" in the Third Millenium.

Globalisation and the rights and employment condiitons of teachers and education personnel

The Third World Congress of Education International, meeting in Jomtien, Thailand, from 25 to 29 July, 2001:

1. *Recognising* the reality of globalisation brings both challenges and opportunities but that in terms of

impact current patterns of globalisation, driven by powerful economic forces, governments and international institutions, threaten the working conditions of education personnel by introducing a neo-liberal model to dismantle the welfare state and move to a competitive state by privatising education;

2. *Concerned* at attempts to change education from a human right provided through public service for the collective good to a commodity to be acquired for private advantage;

3. *Recognising* that pressure is required at the national and international levels to oppose the inclusion of education in the General Agreement of Trade in Services (GATS) and to ensure that the policies of the World Trade Organisation(WTO), the World Bank and the International Monetary Fund (IMF) acknowledge public education as a human right;

4. *Noting* that the 2001 report of the Committee of Experts on the application of the ILO/UNESCO Recommendation on the Status of Teachers (CEART) states There has been a tremendous expansion of education against a background of pauperisation of teaching and learning conditions creating an environment unattractive to potential recruits and to teachers currently in service.

5. *Acknowledging* that demands for predictability, account-ability, flexibility, and efficiency have led to new forms of management in education and have resulted in a deterioration of working conditions and relationships in education;

6. *Recognising* the increasing importance of international unionism to organise and campaign effectively for

patterns of globalisation that is human rights based, people-oriented and based on mutual help and solidarity;

7. *Concerned* at the levels of stress and burnout in education workers;

8. Congress recommends that EI and its member organisations shall;

   a) Extend union membership to include all education personnel if appropriate;

   b) Organise education personnel on part-time and temporary contracts as well as those working in the non-formal education system if appropriate;

   c) Demand the trade union rights guaranteed in international human rights instruments for all education personnel;

   d) Promote and pilot new patterns of organisation in education to provide more job satisfaction through empowerment of education personnel;

   e) Negotiate for the support services necessary to provide quality education;

   f) Shape the use of new technology as a tool to help with the learning process to educate people;

   g) Negotiate the right to and the terms for participation in decision making at all levels of education;

   h) Explore collegial approaches to team work that give team members different responsibilities;

   i) Negotiate terms of employment that reward those who choose to continue working directly with students instead of opting for management positions;

j) Challenge the time-consuming bureaucratic tasks that are required of educators;

k) Negotiate time for preparation, planning and team consultation for staff;

l) Negotiate salaries, entitlements and conditions of work commensurate with those with similar qualifications and responsibilities in other sectors and that are sufficient to fully accomplish their professional responsibilities;

m) Ensure quality training programmes, both initial and in-service, are available to all education personnel at times that make it possible for all education personnel to take advantage of the programmes.

n) Lower the number of students per class to improve the success of students;

o) Improve the working environment of education personnel through provision of functional institutions with modern equipment and improved, relevant pedagogical materials;

p) Make teaching a more attractive profession by reversing the trend to lower the status and recognise the increasing difficulty of the work:

q) Support teacher exchange among countries but avoid the brain drain of qualified teachers by wealthier countries;

r) Promote equality of rights between men and women, particularly concerning salary, working conditions and entitlements;

s) Oppose the fragmentation and disintegration of formal collective bargaining and the resulting variation in conditions of service;

t) Demand the establishment of appropriate collective bargaining and dispute resolution mechanisms for all education employees.

Gender perspective in development cooperation

The Third World Congress of Education International, meeting in Jomtien, Thailand, from 25 to 29 July, 2001:

1. *Recalls* that the constitution commits EI "to combat all forms of racism and of bias or discrimination in education and society due to gender, marital status, sexual orientation, age, religion, political opinion, social or economic status or national or ethnic origin";

2. *Recognises* EI's commitment to promoting the equality of men and women, of boys and girls in society, in education and in the trade union movement and supports the efforts of EI in reinforcing the participation of women in EI's activities through, among other strategies, the use of quotas for women's participation;

3. *Notes* that while the majority of members of EI member organizations are women, fewer women than men hold positions of responsibility in teacher unions;

4. *Recognises* that the economic conditions of women are lower than those of men, and that structural adjustment policies applied through neoliberalism

have worsened the status of women, who are today more vulnerable;

5. *Recognises* also that women do not truly benefit from the same opportunities as men in any part of the world and that they continue to struggle for equality, respect, dignity, development and peace, equity in healthcare, social security, well-being needed to recover self-esteem;

6. *Recalls* the UNICEF report on the State of the World's Children, 1999 and the Beijing Platform highlight the lack of educational opportunities for women and girls;

7. *Notes* that the Second World Congress of Education International determined that EI and member organizations shall establish a work programme in each region to, among other things, ensure that a gender analysis is an integral part of all research and analysis done by EI

8. *Recalls* the EI development cooperation policy adopted by the 2nd World Congress which notes that development cooperation draws on the concepts of independence, promotion of democracy, of quality public education services for all, increasing autonomy, gender equity, sustainable development, long-term planning and mutual respect;

9. *Recognises* the importance of the current EI and member organisations' development cooperation programmes in increasing the participation of women in education unions and in their employment as educators;

10. *Recognises* that while development projects improve conditions and leadership opportunities for women

in the teacher unions and education communities, more programmes are needed to ensure effective gender equality over the long term;

11. *Recognises* further that successful gender projects and other projects that are oriented towards the improvement of women's rights in development cooperation enable women to share among themselves but also enable them to represent their interests in the mainstream of the union, the community and their country;
12. *Recognises* the extreme importance of promoting sustainability of women's programmes;
13. *Acknowledges* that in regard to gender projects in development cooperation, training for the union leadership as well as the grassroots is required in order to achieve sustainability and to mainstream not marginalised women's issues;
14. The Congress determines that EI and its member organizations must, in monitoring the work on gender and development cooperation, commit to:
    - — Support the continuing need for projects and programmes on gender issues, targeted at women and other projects and programmes, aimed at improving the rights and the role of women, and not only targeted at them;
    - — Lobby towards governments in order to improve the economic, social and educational conditions of women and girls;
    - — Provide gender awareness training and training on other issues of concern to women for union leaders, union staff and women at continental,

national, regional and local levels and contribute to the increasing participation of women in positions of responsibility by looking for means to reconcile trade union responsibilities and family life;

— Develop a gender analysis instrument to assess the overall impact of proposed programmes and projects and ensure that such analysis is undertaken for all development cooperation project proposals;
— Incorporate an analysis of the current situation of the union to provide a basis for evaluation of the project outcomes, in particular, sustainability;
— Include indicators of quality and sustainability as well as quantifying measures in project evaluation and measures of project effectiveness;
— Carry on the campaigns for full protection of maternity, breast-feeding, and care of pre-school children;
— Include on the negotiation agendas of EI member organisations, issues of concern specifically to women;
— Stimulate the development of curricula that promote non sexist education;
— Dedicate larger ressources to the development of projects for women;
— Strengthen and consolidate the networks of women educators per region, and move on with regional plans to ensure that experiences are shared, both in instances where gender and

development has made progress and where it is only just starting to boost initiatives in each organisation.

Transnational provison of higher education

The Third World Congress of Education International meeting in Jomtien, Thailand, from 25 to 29 July 2001:

A. Notes:

1. The growth of provision of higher education across national borders, utilizing mainly internet-based technologies, by traditional universities as well as by solely on-line providers;
2. The participation by a number of universities in joint ventures with for-profit corporations and other higher education institutions for the provision of higher education relying on internet-based materials and technologies;
3. Growing concern among higher education personnel, students and the communities they work with regarding the lack of clear and unambiguous information available in relation to governance structures, quality assurance and accreditation procedures, and employment practices within such joint ventures;

B. Believes that:

4. Predominantly on-line higher education providers should be subject to rigorous quality assurance mechanisms to ensure a curriculum developed, taught and under academic control of faculty who have tenure and academic freedom, and this principle should be reflected in international accreditation procedures;

5. It is the responsibility of national governments, international organisations and higher education providers to ensure that the expansion of web-based transnational higher education provision is informed by public interest concerns and objectives, and not solely by profit motives or market forces;

Accordingly, EI *should:*

6. Encourage higher education trade unions to develop strategies for actively organising members across national boundaries to ensure that the employment rights of personnel employed by transnational providers are protected;
7. In conjunction with higher education unions that have already undertaken significant work in this area, develop guidelines for best practice in relation to the provision of transnational education and actively pursue their endorsement and implementation by UNESCO, the ILO, the World Trade Organisation and international accreditation bodies, such implementation to be pursed in conjonction with EI.

   Such guidelines should address, among other issues, governance structures, quality assurance, the importance of culturally relevant content and modes of delivery, accreditation, intellectual property management and academic freedom.

Status of higher education Personnel

The Third World Congress of Education International, meeting in Jomtien, Thailand, from 25 to 29 July, 2001:

A. Education International affirms:

1. The rights and freedoms of higher education teaching personnel as defined in the UNESCO Recommendation concerning the Status of Higher Education Teaching Personnel;

2. The important role all higher education personnel play in contributing, through their work, to the dissemination of knowledge, the furthering of social and economic goals, and the pursuit of innovation and new ideas;

3. The responsibility of personnel working in higher education institutions to work towards making the benefits of higher education available to all;

B. However, Education International notes:

4. An erosion in academic freedom, particularly in terms of academics' right to engage in teaching, research and scholarship without interference, and their responsibility to promote the work of the university as critic and conscience of society;

C. Education International believes that this is the product of a number of converging factors, including:

5. The increasing reliance of universities around the world on corporate and other forms of private funding;

6. The erosion of tenure and other forms of oNGOing employment;

7. The failure of national governments to observe and give substance to the rights and freedoms of higher education personnel as endorsed in the UNESCO Recommandation;

8. The absence to date of a report from the Director General on the world situation with regard to

academic freedom, as required by Article 75 of the UNESCO Recommandation;

D. Therefore, Education International should:

9. Continue to engage in discussions with the ILO as to how the rights and freedoms expressed in the UNESCO Recommandation concerning the Status of Higher Education Teaching Personnel might be promoted and protected in international agreements, and to protect the rights and freedoms of all higher education personnel;

10. Organise a conference involving representatives of EI affiliates, national governments, and NGO's (including UNESCO) to review implementation of the document (including the publication of reports on academic freedom from Member States) and formulate a strategy to ensure that it has wider efficacy.

Situation of Colombian educators

The Third World Congress of Education International, meeting in Jomtien, Thailand, from 25 to 29 July, 2001:

1. Recalls that, as set out in Article 2(b) of the Constitution of Education International, one of the organisation's objectives is to promote peace, democracy, social justice and equality among all peoples and nations, and to promote the implementation of the Universal Declaration of Human Rights through the development of education and the collective strength of teachers and education workers;

2. Notes the Vienna Declaration and the Action Programme adopted following the UN Conference on

Human Rights, which state that human rights and fundamental civil liberties are inherent in all human beings and that protecting and promoting these rights and freedoms is the first responsibility of governments;

3. Highlights and denounces the fact that since 1987 Colombian educators have been subjected to all manner of political persecution and attacks against their trade unions, and have been the victims of numerous "disappearances" and murders; more specifically, that to date 433 teachers have been murdered or have disappeared and more than 1,000 have had to leave their homes under threat of death, and that in the first few months of 2001 seven of our colleagues have already fallen victim to the wave of violence unleashed against teachers in Colombia;

4. Denounces and rejects the repressive policies—aimed at quashing social protest—which the Colombian government under the leadership of the President of the Republic, Andrés Pastrana AraNGO, has been implementing against Colombian workers in general and teachers in particular;

In view of the above, the Congress recommends that Education International and its member organisations:

5. Uphold the human rights of all teachers;

6. Convey to Colombia's leaders their condemnation of the wave of persecution and assassinations;

7. Urge the Colombian government to condemn and reject the persecution and murder of Colombian educators and to take effective measures to guarantee the free exercise of the teaching profession and of trade union activity.

Situation in the Former Yugoslovian republic of macedona

The Third World Congress of Education International, meeting in Jomtien, Thailand, from 25 to 29 July, 2001:

1. Cannot condone demands for political rights through the use of force and terror. Therefore, the Congress strongly supports the legal authorities of FYR Macedonia in their attempt at settling all open issues through dialogue. In this respect, the Congress also urges international institutions, such as the UN, the Council of Europe, the EU and NATO, to continue giving the necessary support to the democratically elected leadership of FYR Macedonia so that it can find a quick solution to the current crisis;

2. Bearing in mind that these unwanted events have an extremely negative influence on the development of FYR Macedonia, particularly on the development of and reforms in the education sector and the living conditions of workers and all citizens, pledges that the Education International will undertake all necessary measures and activities, including calling upon international financial organisations and EI affiliates worldwide to extend material and financial assistance and other forms of benefits to their colleagues in FYR Macedonia so that they can overcome the current crisis more quickly and easily;

3. Calls on the Macedonian government to recognise and accept the rights of indigenous Albanian Macedonians to learn in their mother tongue in schools and to participate in public administration in Macedonia;

4. Encourages the EI affiliate in the country to continue its activities before the competent state bodies for re-establishing normal conditions for continuation of education in all the schools located in the affected regions.

Resolution on trafficking in women girls and boys

The Third World Congress of Education International, meeting in Jomtien, Thailand, from 25 to 29 July, 2001:

1. *Noting* that trafficking in women and girls has become one of the fastest growing criminal enterprises in the world affecting all nations;
2. *Further* noting that an estimated two million women and girls are trafficked annually around the world, for the purpose of forced labor, domestic servitude or sexual exploitation;
3. *Concerned* that traffickers in women and girls, like narcotic traffickers, operate boldly across international borders, using modern means of communication and trade to lure victims with false promises as well as using force, deception, and coercion to enslave victims;
4. *Outraged* that well-established criminal organizations traffic in women, girls and boys capitalising on increased poverty, rising unemployment and disintegrating social networks in developing countries;
5. *Noting* that Europe, North America, the Gulf States, India and Asia are important destination points for trafficking victims;

6. *Appalled* that increasingly very young children are being trafficked because of fear of contracting HIV/AIDS;

The Third World Congress of Education International calls on governments to:

7. *combat* trafficking in women, girls and boys through public awareness campaigns that provide information on the means traffickers use to lure young women, girls and boys who are then forced into prostitution;
8. *ensure* that sufficient funds are available to provide law enforcement agencies with the means necessary to combat trafficking and to prosecute traffickers to the full extent of the law;
9. *enact* "long reach laws' that will allow for the trial in the country of origin of any person charged with soliciting an underage child;
10. *treat* women, girls and boys who are victims of trafficking as victims and to provide support, counselling and training to them to be able to leave prostitution and to support themselves;
11. *provide* free compulsory education for children and to provide the necessary transitional services for children to be able to attend school and support themselves.

Resolution on Burma

The Third World Congress of Education International, meeting in Jomtien, Thailand, from 25 to 29 July, 2001:

1. *Notes* with concern the systematic and increasingly severe violations of civil, political, economic, social and cultural rights in Burma;

2. *Condemns* the military government for not convening the National Convention since 1996 in order to implement its commitment to the international community to take the steps necessary to recognise the democratically elected government headed by Aung San Suu Kyi;
3. *Notes* the increased repression of any form of public political activity along with the systematic surveillance of those exercising their rights to freedom of thought, expression, assembly and association as well as the harassment of their families;
4. *Deplores* the fact that multinational companies support dictatorship in Burma through their activities in the country;
5. *Deplores* the continued extra-judicial, summary and arbitrary executions, torture and abuse of women and children by government agents;
6. *Further deplores* the imposition of oppressive measures directed at ethnic and religious minorities;
7. *Condemns* the violations of human rights including systematic programmes of forced relocation directed against ethnic minorities as well as the use of forced labour, trafficking, sexual violence and exploitation, committed by military personnel and especially directed at women who are returning refugees, the internally displaced, members of ethnic minorities or members of the political opposition;
8. *Equally condemns* the severe restrictions on all forms of domestic media and international publications;
9. *Deeply concerned* at violations of the rights of children and youth including lack of access to schools and the closure for over three years of most higher education institutions;

The Third World Congress of Education International:

10. *Calls* on the United Nations to insist that the military government of Burma implement the recommendations of the UN Special Rapporteur on Burma, as well as encouraging UN Member States to implement the resolution on Burma adopted by the 2001 ILO General Conference;
11. *Requests* the Economic and Social Council of the United Nations to hold a special session to outline the steps to be taken to get the military government of Burma to conform to UN resolutions;
12. *Urges* EI member organisations to lobby their government and the WTO to insist that WTO procedures cannot be used to stop countries wishing to impose sanctions on Burma because of its human rights violations;
13. *Urges* EI member organisations to ask their governments to support activities that will assist Burmese refugees and in particular to provide opportunities for education for Burmese students;
14. *Encourages* EI member organisations to include programmes to assist the refugees on the Thai/ Burmese border in the provision of education programmes;
15. *Calls* on EI member organisations to undertake a programme at the national level to raise awareness of the plight of Burmese citizens and to support initiatives, including unrestricted communication and access to Aung San Suu Kyi and other leaders of the National League for Democracy, to ensure respect for the ILO Convention on Forced Labour, UN Convention on the Rights of the Child and other human rights instruments.

Situation in Nepal

The Third World Congress of Education International, meeting in Jomtien, Thailand, from 25 to 29 July, 2001:

1. *Expresses* solidarity with the affiliated trade unions (NNTA and NTA) and the Nepalese people following the assassination of the royal family;

2. *Regrets* having been forced to transfer the venue of the present World Congress from Kathmandu to Jomtien for obvious security reasons, which continue to apply, and having thus missed the opportunity of showing to the global community of trade union educators the economic, social and cultural reality of a country seeking development;

3. *Stresses* that contemporary history shows that development always goes hand in hand with the democratic and transparent functioning of governmental institutions, to which the population and democratic organisations of civil society must adhere, and that guerilla practices most often delay any possibility of development, owing to the hesitations of potential investors, amongst others;

4. *Recognises* the struggle against poverty which prevents many Nepalese children from participating in formal schooling;

The Third Education International World Congress:

5. *Requests* that the Nepalese government and the organisations part of or supporting the guerilla find a political solution to the present conflict, so that the country returns to peace and stability, which are prerequisites to any development;

6. *Requests* that NNTA and NTA promote an education in favour of civil peace and democracy in a context of social justice. Only political and democratic stability can protect the rights of Nepalese teachers including their personal safety, ensure freedom for Nepalese communities, improve the economic conditions for the citizens of Nepal and promote unity and social justice;
7. *Requests* the Executive Board to take the appropriate initiatives by the next Congress, in collaboration with the Nepalese authorities, international institutions and organisations of the Nepalese society, to promote education for all and to campaign against illiteracy in the framework of the Global Campaign for Education, in order to help reduce poverty.

Resolution on the Situation in Afghanistan

The Third World Congress of Education International, meeting in Jomtien, Thailand, from 25 to 29 July, 2001:

1. *Whereas,* in 1996, after nearly 20 years of invasion, internal strife and civil war, the political and military force known as the Taliban took control of the government of Afghanistan. At the time, many Afghanis welcomed the Taliban in the hope that the new government would bring stability, security and economic relief to Afghanistan. However, in the intervening years the Taliban has failed to meet these aspirations and has established an authoritarian state that has deprived Afghans of their basic human rights;
2. *Whereas,* the 56th session of the year 2000 United Nations Commission on Human Rights "condemned

the widespread violations and abuses of human rights and humanitarian law and the continuing grave violations of the human rights of women and girls, including all forms of discrimination against them;"

3. *Whereas,* human rights organizations report that the Taliban has deliberately and systematically killed thousands of people. Additionally, under Taliban edicts women in Afghanistan have been made virtual prisoners in their own homes; and girls have been prohibited from attending school;
4. *Whereas,* on May 22, 2001 the Taliban ordered Hindu men in Afghanistan to wear yellow cloth badges pinned to their shirt pockets, and Hindu and Sikh women to veil themselves in public as Muslin women are required to do;
5. *Resolved,* that the Education International most stongly condemns the continuing violations of human and political rights carried out by the Taliban movement in Afghanistan. We especially note the actions by the Taliban that have virtually eliminated any rights, including the right to education, for women and girls in Afghanistan;
6. *Resolved,* that the Education International strongly condemns the action by the Taliban to require Hindu men to wear yellow badges. This is an extreme example of racism and human rights violation reminiscent of Nazi Germany. Historically, such actions have been part of systematic actions to expel or eliminate entire categories of national minorities;
7. *Resolved,* that the Education International calls on the United Nations and other appropriate governmental and non-governmental institutions and organizations

to expose all continuing violations of human rights on the part of the Taliban and to take all possible actions to end these extreme violations of human rights by the Taliban against the people of Afghanistan.

Resolution on the Situation in Palestine

The Third World Congress of Education International, meeting in Jomtien, Thailand, from 25 to 29 July, 2001:

1. *Notes* with concern the dangerous escalation of the Israelo-Palestinian conflict, the principal victims of which are children, owing to the non-application of the UN resolutions and to the non-respect of the peace agreements signed between the two parties;
2. *Considers* the appeals for peace launched by the international community;
3. *Acknowledges* the wish of the Israeli teacher trade union (ITU) to open a dialogue with the Palestinian trade union leaders;
4. *Acknowledges* the role played by the Palestinian teacher trade union (GUPT) to support peace and justice;
5. *Calls for*
   a) the ending of all violence and the immediate application of the ceasefire without preconditions;
   b) the end of colony settlements on Palestinian territories;
   c) the resumption of the negociations in search of a global, equitable and sustainable peace on the basis of the agreements reached and the recognition of the legitimate rights of the two people recognised by the UN;

d) all pupils and students to be able to attend school and university safely;

6. *Decides* to send an EI delegation to investigate the conditions of teachers and students in the Palestinian territories and in Israel;

7. *Decides* to organise an international conference of the Arab teacher trade unions affiliated to EI;

8. *Decides* to continue to organise, as shortly as possible, the conference, including peace and justice, entitled Learning to Live Together.

Revision of Distribution of History in Japanese Textbooks

The Third World Congress of Education International, meeting in Jomtien, Thailand, from 25 to 29 July, 2001:

1. *Concerned* that some Japanese history textbooks for middle schools edited under the initiative of Japanese right-wing groups were authorised by the Japanese government. Such outcome would damage the friendly relations among countries of the Asia-Pacific area and, moreover, have a negative influence on history that they promote and other inappropriate contents such as the glorification of the Japanese colonial rule and history of aggression. Therefore, we wish to declare the following;

2. *Reminds* the Japanese government that these days the international trend is to reflect on one's own history of wars and violence and make efforts to create a new peaceful age, as demonstrated by Germany, for example, which has made a grave reflection of its history and given good apologies and compensations

to war victims. We further urge the government to (1) immediately correct such history textbooks that glorify its wars and colonial rule while distorting the historical truth and (2) positively participate in the international trend to bring about peace;

3. *Urges* the Japanese government to faithfully implement the UNESCO Recommendations (Education for Inter-national Understanding, Cooperation, and Peace and that for Liberty of Human and Fundamental Rights. Nov 19, 1974) stating that education should contribute to respect for the fundamental liberty and human rights, establishment of social justice, and promotion of international understanding and world peace and also objection activities against all kinds of neo-colonialism, all forms of racism and fascism, and other ideologies arousing ethnical and racial hatred;
4. *Urges* the Japanese government to alter the procedure of selecting and adopting textbooks so as to allow reflection of reasonable opinions gathered from teachers and their associations, who are the subject of education;
5. *Demands* that the Japanese government settle complications arising with associated countries and develop cooperative relationships through immediate truthful history education based on the universal values pursued by mankind.

Resolution on the Situation in Algeria

The Third World Congress of Education International, meeting in Jomtien, Thailand, from 25 to 29 July, 2001:

1. *Alarmed* by the serious political and social situation in Algeria where the denial of civic liberties and democratic rights has been accompanied in the last few weeks by organised violence against young people and teachers, resulting in the deaths of more than 100 people. So far the government has ignored the social, political and cultural demands claims voiced in mass demonstrations;

2. *Noting* that this dramatic situation is fuelled by the incapacity of the government of using the country's wealth in the development, education and training of young people;

3. *Urges* the Algerian authorities to:

   a) Put an end to repression, which can only aggravate the crisis;

   b) Make every effort to bring about a democratic solution based on free debate, the rule of law, respect for cultural diversity, and the right to education and health care;

   c) Enable the free exercise of basic civic liberties (freedom of association and expression and freedom to organise demonstrations);

   d) Facilitate, without any restrictions, the activities of national and international human rights and trade union organisations;

4. *Urges* the international community to help Algeria overcome this serious crisis;

5. *Wishes* to express its solidarity with, and support for its member union in Algeria, the SATEF, which should be allowed to freely express its views, act and negotiate with the authorities everywhere in the country.

Resolution on Violence, Education and the Peace Process in Sri Lanka

The Third World Congress of Education International, meeting in Jomtien, Thailand, from 25 to 29 July, 2001:

1. *Noting* that the international airport of Sri Lanka was been on fire on 24th July 2001, having being attacked by rebels with knowledge and skills;
2. *Further noting* that Sri Lanka has a literacy record of about 92 per cent but recalling that education for all cannot be achieved successfully without wisdom and peace, i.e what is happening to Sri Lanka today may happen to any other country;
3. *Requests* the Sri Lankan government to expedite the peace process mediated by Norway with the support of the International community especially by the United States of America, the United Kingdom and India to find out a political solution to the ethnic issue in Sri Lanka;
4. *Requests* EI to pay more attention to the subject of loving kindness to inject mindfulness and wisdom to the future humanity to live in peace and prosperity.

Resolution on the Imprisonment of Education Trade Union Leaders in Korea

The Third World Congress of Education International, meeting in Jomtien, Thailand, from 25 to 29 July, 2001:

1. *Noting* that in Korea, only private school owners can decide on budget matters and the settlement of accounts, although teachers' salaries and expenses related to the management of schools are paid for by

the national treasury. As a result, the work of some schools has been disrupted. The Ministry of Education does not pay attention to any of these matters;

2. *Further noting* that KTU organized a mass rally and its leaders went on a hunger strike in the month of June, during which two KTU leaders were detained;

3. *Demands* the release of those two detained teachers who were arrested during the demonstration against the corrupted private schools and also urges the Korean government to revise the private school laws.

Resolution on the Solidarity with the Teachers Affected by the Earthquake in South Peru

The Third World Congress of Education International, meeting in Jomtien, Thailand, from 25 to 29 July, 2001:

Considering:

1. That, on Saturday 23 June 2001, the villages in the South of Peru were hit by an earthquake of a magnitude of 7° on the Richter scale. The earthquake has caused the death, ruin and despair of the inhabitants of this part of the country;

2. That this fact is far worse for the villages in the centre of the country, whose road infrastructure has been seriously damaged, preventing help from being given appropriately. Dozens of villages are isolated, families have lost their houses and homes, their crops have been ruined;

3. That the teachers in the South of Peru have lost their houses, and their schools have been seriously affected;

The Third World Congress of Education International wishes to:

4. *Express* its solidarity with the Peruvian people and with the teachers in particular;
5. *Request* that all the teachers in the world join the world campaign to support the people and in particular the teachers in Peru;
6. *Seek* the immediate attention of the Peruvian Government as well as the rehabilitation of the villages affected by the earthquake.

Resolution on the Solidarity with SUTEP and the Peruvian People for having defeated the dictatorship of Fujimori and Montesinos

The Third World Congress of Education International, meeting in Jomtien, Thailand, from 25 to 29 July, 2001:

Considering:

1. That, since the beginning of the 1990s, Peru has been victimised by one of the dictatorships in South America, to apply the neoliberal model most unconditionally. In fact, the Fujimori regime restructured society, applied economic reforms and modified the legislation in direct favour of transnational capital, rendering the teachers, the workers, and the people defenseless and poor;
2. That, since April 1992, this regime was in power following a coup disrupting the Republican Congress, Public Authority, Judicial Authority and the means of communication, and installed with the complicity of the leaders of the armed forces a fierce

dictatorship persecuting the opposition and the democratic sectors such as SUTEP;

3. That, the regime, in its intent to seize power for two or more presidential terms, changed into an officially democratic regime, but in reality became a corrupt dictatorship. The Fujimori and Montesinos criminals killed while remaining unpunished, plundered the country's resources, and overexploited its workers. And as if that was not enough, they repressed the people mercilessly, and from their position of power engaged in arms and drugs trafficking;

4. That the dictatorship had as one of its objectives the privatisation of public education and imposed the "recommendations" of the International Monetary Fund and the World Bank, which in the long run have accelerated the deterioration of public education. At this point SUTEP, representing 285,000 teachers, had to defend firmly quality public education as well as the necessity to develop a national plan on education, which would put education back on its tracks.

5. That, especially in the last two years, the main fighting strategy of the Peruvians has been the utmost unity of action to defeat the dictatorship. In this process, SUTEP has played a crucial and decisive role. At the end of 2000, the corrupt regime was thrown out by the people. Today, Vladimiro Montesinos is imprisoned, and Alberto Fujimori, the other major criminal, is protected by the Japanese Government;

6. That the actions of the dictatorship not only have affected the economy, the productive structure and the agriculture, resulting in the fact that an

unprecedented 50.7 per cent of the population now lives in poverty; but the dictatorship has also institutionalised corruption, blackmail and immorality, affecting the whole society;

In conclusion, the Third Education International World Congress Wishes:

7. To express its solidarity with SUTEP and the Peruvian people in their democratic and antidictatorial fight which has defeated the dictatorship of Fujimori and Montesinos and restored the democracy in Peru;
8. To urge the elected Government to implement from 28 July of this year, the readjustment of its political economy so as to help respond to the needs of the country;
9. The respect and validation of quality public education, converting it into a state affair with the fundamental strategic aim of developing the country;
10. The just punishment of the accused Vladimir Montesinos and the just extradition judgement and conviction of Alberto Fujimori;
11. Support for and solidarity with SUTEP's fight to achieve professional, economic, social, cultural and labour rights, towards the success of a National Education Project.

Resolution on the International Labour Organisation, the World Trade Organisation and the Globalisation of the Economy

The Third World Congress of Education International, meeting in Jomtien, Thailand, from 25 to 29 July, 2001:

1. *Recognising* the dramatic increase in world trade and foreign investment and the impact on citizens resulting from the globalisation of the world economy;

2. *Noting* the intensification of the liberalisation of trade since the establishment of the World Trade Organisation;

3. *Concerned* at the impact on workers' jobs, pay, conditions of employment and the pressures to limit the bargaining strength of trade unions by powerful transnational financial institutions prepared to increase the disparity within societies by forcing down wages and worsening employment conditions;

4. *Concerned* also at the pressures on governments to privatise education, healthcare and other public services;

5. *Supporting* the expansion of trade and investment, provided that the objective is to stimulate growth, to help end world poverty, to raise the living standards of all peoples and to ensure environmentally sustainable development;

6. *Welcomes* the existence of, and recognises the need for, international economic and financial institutions. However, Congress calls upon governments, especially those constituting the G8 Group, to require these institutions to be more open and democratic in their procedures, in setting their aims and in establishing their priorities;

7. *Believes* that greater public awareness and a more informed debate would prove beneficial to all the interests concerned;

8. *Convinced* that the right of access to markets confers the responsibility to ensure that the workers' basic rights are universally respected, that the State's capacity to develop public services such as education is not impeded, that production and distribution of cultural works are especially protected and that protection of the environment is respected;
9. *Welcomes* the consensus reached at the UN World Summit for Social Development, including the specific reference to the importance of respect for the seven basic international labour standards, to make progress in the reduction of poverty and unemployment;
10. *Supports* the work done by ICFTU and ITSs to find ways to ensure observance of international labour standards within international trade agreements and notes, with appreciation, the work of TUAC on the Multilateral Agreement on Investment (MAI) while stating principled opposition to this agreement;
11. *Calls* on the World Trade Organisation to take into account the efforts of governments, trade unions, employers and international organisations like the ILO to raise standards by implementing the ILO Conventions;
12. *Urges* the WTO and the ILO to establish a joint working group on Trade and Labour Standards to examine how core labour standards can be integrated into trade agreements, to determine operating mechanisms and means of co-operation between the WTO and the ILO;
13. *Believes* that the free market model, which underpins the WTO's trade liberalisation program, is inappropriate for education;

14. Congress calls on EI and its member organisations to:

- *Work* with the ICFTU and the ITSs to encourage the governments and employers on the Working Party of the ILO Governing Body on the Social Dimensions of the Liberalisation of International Trade to enter into dialogue with the Worker's Group to consider how the procedures of the WTO can be adapted to promote the observance of core ILO Conventions;
- *Publicise* among member organisations information to raise awareness of violations of standards by companies, particularly when child labour or forced or bonded labour are involved, or where workers are refused the right to organise;
- *Promote*—through the trade unions in different parts of the world—a new approach to the processes of regional integration. We must devise new organisational strategies for Mercosur, NAFTA, the European Union, the Central American Market, the Organisation of African Unity, and the various regional organisations in Asia;
- *Oppose*, through strategically planned actions, WTO plans which result in increasing poverty, concen-trating wealth in the hands of a minority, and preventing the emergence of genuine programmes for health, education and scientific and technological development, geared to creating a more responsible and caring world;

— *Promote* the creation of negotiating bodies in each country to enable the trade unions to discuss the new framework which all these changes as a whole imply for working conditions and education;
— *Encourage* member organisations and their members to support companies that respect core labour standards in the production of their products and support initiatives to promote social labelling;
— *Participate* in the trade and labour standards discussions with the ICFTU, at the ILO and through TUAC atthe OECD;
— *Focus* specific attention on encouraging EI member organisations to lobby their governments to support strengthening the mandate of the ILO to deal with countries that consistently violate the core labour standards;
— *Continue* to work to promote the inclusion of core labour standards in trade agreements;

15. Congress also calls on EI and its member organisations to campaign for education, health care, and social services generally to be excluded from the scope of the WTO's General Agreement on Trade in Services (GATS). Consistent with this objective, EI and its member organisations should:

— *Demand* full openness and transparency of GATS negotiations e.g. publication of government mandates, consultation with national and international union organisations, publication of reports and projects on trade in services discussed within the OECD and regional trade groupings;

- *Oppose* proposals to transform GATS into a comprehensive top-down agreement, thereby placing the onus on countries to secure exemptions for particular services;
- *Support* the right of national governments to regulate the provision of education, such as culturally appropriate content for courses and qualifications, the licensing of schools and universities, and the supply of tertiary places in particular discipline areas and the number of corresponding schools or faculties where viability is a consideration;
- *Collect* information on the consequences of GATS to date, and establish links with campaigns by non-government organisations concerned about the GATS;
- *Oppose* the development of new GATS disciplines that would allow for WTO dispute-panels to judge whether technical standards and licensing and qualification requirements and procedures affecting education and other social services are too 'trade-restrictive';
- *Oppose* the development of new GATS disciplines that limit the rights of national governments to determine the allocation of government subsidies to education and social service providers.

Higher education and research policy

The Third World Congress of Education International meeting in Jomtien, Thailand, from 25 to 29 July 2001:

A. Affirms EI's commitment to the continuing development of higher education and research noting that:

1. Higher education institutions play a central educational, economic and employment role in society, in scientific, technological and applied research and through the production of skilled graduates (including primary and secondary teachers);
2. Strong higher education and research institutions underpin a vibrant and pluralistic civil society, and enrich social and cultural life by generating new knowledge and by continuously enhancing humanity's intellectual and cultural heritage;
3. Higher education is often an important focus of resistance to authoritarian regimes, and plays a significant role in promoting human rights, democracy and cultural and intellectual tolerance;

B. Considers that the development of higher education and research should be guided by the following principles and priorities:

4. The importance of a strong, public higher education sector to ensure that access to lifelong learning is available to all citizens;
5. Access to and participation in higher education should be available to all that meet relevant entry criteria and should not be limited by the financial means or social origins of students. This means that higher education, as well as other education sectors, should be free of charge, and that the State should ensure that adequately funded student support schemes are available. Where fees do apply, they should not exceed 20 per cent of total course costs and appropriate subsidies, grants and options for deferred repayment must be available;

6. Funding for universities, colleges and research institutions is primarily the responsibility of the State, and the State should maintain its overriding responsibility for ensuring that higher education and research institutions serve the public interest. Where private institutions exist and receive State support, they should be required to adhere to the same standards and levels of accountability as public institutions;

7. While the State has a right and an obligation to insist on public accountability from higher education and research institutions for the expenditure of public funds such accountability should not undermine institutional autonomy in relation to academic policies, curriculum, staff appointments and internal management. Institutional autonomy, in these spheres, is a precondition for the existence of academic freedom. This in turn guarantees that independent research, teaching and scholarship can flourish;

8. An essential element of academic freedom is the right of staff to be directly represented on all key decision-making bodies within universities, colleges and research institutions and for decision-making to reflect collegial principles. Collective decision-making must guarantee and develop individual staff rights such as the freedom to determine teaching style or the right to intellectual property;

9. Research and scholarship is guaranteed and underwritten by the existence of academic tenure or job security. Universities and colleges should provide tenured opportunities through appropriate policies or collective agreements. Member States of UNESCO

should be encouraged to adhere to the terms of the UNESCO Recommendation Concerning the Status of Higher Education Teaching Personnel and to adopt positive measures for its speedy implementation. Where staff are not employed in tenured posts but on shorter term contracts, their industrial and professional rights should be equivalent to those of tenured colleagues;

C. Welcomes the progress made in the higher education and research sector since the Harare Congress, particularly in the following areas:

10. the significant increase in affiliations by unions representing higher education and research staff;
11. the major Conference organised jointly with UNESCO in Paris in March 1997;
12. the substantial work done on the UNESCO Recommendation Concerning the Status of Higher Education Teaching Personnel;

D. Considers that this work should be continued with a particular focus on:

— international cooperation in the areas of higher education and research;

— the democratisation of access to higher education in conjunction with the trend toward mass

— provision of higher education;

— the promotion of students' social status;

— the professionalisation of higher education;

— the world-wide financial crisis in higher education (particularly in the developing world);

— the threats to the academic freedom and working conditions of higher education and research staff;

Expanded EI *work should aim to:*

13. *Strengthen* EI's membership base in the higher education and research sector, and build networks in the sector globally and regionally;

14. *Achieve* and promote the adoption and implementation by National Governments of the UNESCO Recommendation Concerning the Status of Higher Education Teaching Personnel, and develop an effective monitoring process for its implementation;

15. *Defend* higher education budgets from domestic and international threats in the context of a broader international defence of all education sectors. Opposition to international institutions' attempts to deregulate and privatise education is a central element of this defence;

16. *Develop* EI's policies on the role of universities and colleges in teacher education, on lifelong learning, on the implications of new technology and on the links between education and the economy;

17. *Support* academic freedom and the right to collective bargaining including the protection of intellectual property rights and the defence of contract and part-time staff;

18. *Promote* open and accountable institutional governance and management systems and the appropriate involvement of staff unions;

19. *Strengthen* the input of developing countries into the higher education and research work of EI including its regional structures;

20. *Develop* formally structured higher education and research forums as part of regular EI Regional Conferences and prior to the convening of World Congress Meetings;

21. *Ensure* that EI's higher education and research policies are fully covered in EI's dialogue, co-operative work and advocacy with the relevant international and regional bodies and institutions, to ensure that EI's influence within the higher education and research sector is maximised.

3

Knowledge-based Curriculum

The exponential expansion in new information and communication technologies is one result of the general process towards digitisation. What is emerging is the capacity for the convergence of telecommunications, computer and audio-visual technologies 'previously separated by techniques, legislation and modes of distribution'. The convergence between previously distinct forms of communication has organizational and technical consequences.

At the functional level, the once distinct communication media – radio broadcasting, telecommunications and computer technology sectors – have the potential to offer a more hybrid range of services. Radio broadcasting services, for example, will be able to transmit signals other than information or entertainment programmes; the telephone industry will be able to transmit entertainment in addition to conventional services of dialogue and data transmission. At the technical level, old distinctions within the transmission infrastructure (terrestrial broadcasting, cable and satellite) could become obsolete.

Where information is processed in digital form, distribution systems then become multi-purpose. This will undoubtedly have a significant impact on isolated communities and will open up the potential for new and more regular basic education opportunities. The use of new information and communication technologies, and especially of the Internet, has expanded dramatically within the decade. Increasingly, as new technologies are becoming integrated into educational settings, there are new learning opportunities for learners and intermediaries; there is the potential for communicating across geographical distances and time differences with ease, for accessing new pools of information and resources, and for participating in new learning networks and partnerships. In communications, as in every other sector, these developments have been unbalanced. 'Overshadowing the utilization of the new information and communication technologies in education are worldwide disparities in access to these technologies'. Most developing countries lack the basic infrastructure and training needed for gaining access. This 'digital divide' compounds existing inequalities between people within and between countries; the disparities in access are not random but correlate strongly with income, education, ethnic origin, location and gender.

Learners from developing countries therefore face additional risks: the concentration of the ownership of communications systems; the dominance of western educational models and market leaders; and exposure to what may be seen as new forms of political, cultural and linguistic colonialism. The English language dominates. It accounts for 85-90 per cent of Internet messages, 80 per cent of websites and 80-85 per cent of all scientific and technical information in abstracted, published or computer-stored form. The consequences may be to downgrade other languages. But, at the same time, the use of English, already the key international language, means that those with some capacity in it have their access to learning widened by the new technologies. The development of the Internet therefore poses difficult ethical challenges. These may bear particularly on aid agencies.

There is a danger that funding to support Internet development may only nurture an illusion of egalitarianism while differences in access to computer communication in fact shore up existing inequalities. Agency investment in this sector has also been criticized as principally helping the communications industry penetrate new markets and set up new dependencies. Aid for Internet development might divert funds from more traditional forms of development; the balance between funding for books and teachers and funding for technology is not easy. At the same time there is an obvious downside to decisions against funding Internet growth. One response to the demand for investment in communications technology for education has been the pooling of resources between bilateral and multilateral aid agencies in the form of large-scale, collaborative and sectorwide, capacity-building and training initiatives in telecommunications. Examples include the InfoDev programme (World Bank), the International Programme for the Development of Communications (UNESCO), the Intergovernmental Informatics Programme (UNESCO), BellaNet (CIDA, IDRC and UNDP) and the Telecentre Fund (ITU, UNESCO and IDRC). Emphasis has also been placed on innovative ways to develop rural communications, including the notion of developing public access points and resource centres such as community access centres, multi-purpose rural telecentres and public communications booths.

In some developing countries, there have been new opportunities for commercial and small community radio stations to develop educational programming. For example, in some countries of French-speaking West Africa – Benin, Burkina Faso, Guinea, Mali and Senegal – the move away from an exclusively urban-concentrated, government monopoly has resulted in a new wave of community radio programmes for non-formal and adult education, targeted to particular communities and often in a range of African languages.

Audio and video technologies have become cheaper, smaller, more reliable and easier to use. This has made them usable in a wide variety of contexts and by a broader, less professional range of people. Needs-based assessment, discussed in the following section, has given rise to much wider use of audio and video equipment for recording interviews. The media have thus become more accessible to more organizations and individuals working in basic education. Part of this trend can also be seen in the emerging and innovative private sector in rural communication – video rental shops, video recording services for weddings, photocopying, local and long distance telephone shops, fax services, photo-taking, film processing, newspaper and magazine kiosks, book-stores and pre-recorded audio-cassette outlets.

Since the Jomtien conference, most energy and most attention has been given to the expansion of schooling through government action. But this is not the whole story; non-governmental organizations in particular have played a number of roles in the expansion of education and in rethinking approaches to expansion and change.

Although it is difficult to quantify, it seems likely that non-governmental organizations have increased their involvement in basic education, alongside governments. Their work has benefited from their inherent advantages: modest scale, an ability to respond quickly to emergency situations; local knowledge and continuous presence in particular regions. All these have enabled them to make small-scale interventions and target specific, often excluded, populations such women farmers. One consequence of this is a new pattern of co-operation between government agencies and non-governmental organisations in basic education.

People's participation in their own empowerment is critical to foster a sense of dignity and self-reliance. Small and short-term projects may work better than long-term and big projects. Also projects that begin small and then expand carefully have better chances of success. This emphasis on the participation of rural and urban communities in decision-making has led to a proliferation of grass-roots initiatives, and community-based and non-formal education programmes, and has influenced the choice and use of technologies within them. Participatory approaches fit more easily with small-scale, locally developed projects than with those that are centrally planned and rely on broadcasting on a large scale. There is, therefore, a tension between the demand for a participatory approach and attempts to use mass media on the large scale which their technology allows and from which their economic benefits flow. While much non-governmental organization attention has gone to general programmes of basic education, many have also given particular attention to the needs of marginalized basic education groups – girls in some societies, special needs, war children, displaced communities, travellers, street children, adolescents, remote, excluded, religious and ethnic communities. Here, too, in contexts where conventional approaches to basic education have been least successful, the more imaginative projects have benefited from non-govern-mental organizations' freedom of activity and commitment to participatory methodologies. Mainstream status of open and distance learning During the 1990s, open and distance learning moved firmly away from its status as the poor relation and began to be regarded as a legitimate part of mainstream education to be used separately or in combination with face-to-face education. There are now closer links, at all levels, between conventional education and open and distance learning. Another drive towards legitimacy has been the professionalization of open and distance learning – the proliferation of specialist international, regional, and national agencies, organizations, interest groups, professional journals and conferences.

Appropriate use of the technologies is likely to be shaped by changes in the regulatory framework of telecommunications and by insights from new approaches to education that have gained prominence in the past decade. There is a wealth of experience in using technologies to serve the needs of various audiences for basic education. Assessments are difficult as the documentation is scattered and good evaluations are rare. Before looking at the ways in which technologies have been used for different audiences, we examine here the current state of development of the technologies and identify various strategies that have been adopted for their use. Although a theme of much recent discussion of informatics is the convergence of computing and broadcasting technologies, major differences remain between them, at least from the perspective of an educator. Both sets of technologies can be used either to make incremental changes to regular education or to provide access to resources that are not conventionally available to the classroom or to the individual learner. But the ways in which they are used, the challenges they offer to the educator and their different cost structures mean that it makes sense initially to consider them separately.

In schools of high-income countries, a range of educational technologies are taken for granted – audio and videocassette equipment, hand-held still and video cameras, overhead projectors and calculators. These either belong to the school or are on loan from different sources: libraries, local or national educational institutions. Multimedia teaching is encouraged not only by the availability of the technologies, but also by its inclusion within teacher-training courses and by the availability of professional support. In many low- and middle-income countries, by contrast, the dearth of educational technologies is matched by minimal, if any, corresponding teacher training.

International experience makes possible three generalizations: First, where teachers and managers have developed an understanding of multimedia and multi-channel teaching within their own training, they are more likely to adopt innovative ways of securing and using them. Second, planned strategies are required to increase access to educational technologies in schools, particularly low-tech, multimedia resources. Strategies might include government or donor-funded donation initiatives, mobile units, loan systems from libraries and audio-visual resource centres. National and regional audio-visual centres and broadcasting stations in particular emerge as key drivers for producing and introducing audio-visual resources within basic education. Third, we need to understand that infrequent use of technologies within schools may not reflect a lack of training but may be because teachers see little pedagogical value in using them, a factor which techno-enthusiasts overlook.

The Print Media Tools

Continuing literacy requires a literate community, which in turn will enable people to continue learning. The availability of books and other printed material leads to social and political awareness and to continuous self-learning in practical matters such as health, nutrition, agricultural practices and small business operations.

In countries in which the book trade has been destroyed by war or economic collapse, in many countries of Africa, and in remote regions everywhere, the need is great. Henry Chakava, a distinguished Kenyan publisher, has said that 'There is talk in the North about a 'bookless' society, meaning a post-book society, while for us in Africa 'bookless' societies are indeed pre-book societies.'

It is difficult with donor funding to increase access to written materials in everyday life, but funding agencies and civil society organizations are making the effort. The Swedish International Development Co-operation Authority (Sida) has had a broad programme for support of a literate environment, ranging from the supply of Braille presses to workshops for writers of literacy materials and the development and production of supplementary readers, science kits and radio programmes.

It has supported the various links in the book chain, from the collection and publication of oral literature, through writing and publishing, to promotional events such as book weeks and book fairs. It has helped to fund libraries and reading rooms in Botswana, Ethiopia, Mozambique, Nicaragua and the United Republic of Tanzania, language projects in Sierra Leone, Zimbabwe, the Lao People's Democratic Republic and Panama, and authors and authors' organizations such as PEN International.

It has bought and distributed children's books, and has supported libraries, reading campaigns and the training of librarians and teachers in Gaza and the West Bank. It has also supported adult literacy and post-literacy classes, often with accompanying assistance to village reading rooms, rural newspapers, and other materials for new-literates.

In South Asia, with the breakdown of traditional support networks, increased mobility and urbanization, there is increasing demand for literacy. All the countries place an emphasis on primary education and in most of them textbooks are provided free of charge.

In Bangladesh, universal primary education is free and compulsory, and textbooks are supplied to pupils free of charge. Work books, teachers' guides, and other learning materials are, however, reported to be in short supply. Textbooks are written by staff of the National Curriculum and Textbook Board, which also contracts their production and sells them to government. Financial allocations to education rose 46 per cent between 1995/96 and 1999/2000, in part with the help of international loans, and free books were extended to adult literacy centres.

Bangladesh is the only country in South Asia with a national book policy, but the committee entrusted to implement it has never met and the plan remains a blueprint. Books are produced in substantial numbers' some 9,300 textbooks and other educational materials at all levels in 1996' but the quality is poor and most publishers concentrate on the higher secondary and tertiary levels and on cheap guides to passing examinations. Professional skills are not highly developed. Many books are published by the authors themselves. There is no copyright protection and few libraries. Voluntary organizations and civil society organizations promote readership and non-formal education.

In Bhutan, the traditional monastic education is based largely on oral communication and does not support a reading/writing culture, and the fact that English is the official language impedes writing and publishing in the national language, Dzongkha. Bhutan is reported to have published only thirty-two books in 1998. Most of the people who can read are first-generation literates. Supplies of textbooks, work books and teachers' guides are adequate but their printing costs are high and delivery is difficult to remote areas. The government has been providing textbooks free of charge, but in an effort to reduce costs is gradually withdrawing its support for them and stationery from schools in urban and better-off areas.

In Nepal, the educational system penalizes poor families and some prescribed books do not qualify for reimbursement. The curriculum and textbooks are in Nepali, which presents difficulties for the 48 per cent of the population for whom it is not the first language. Textbooks for the public system are produced and distributed by state agencies. Private schools may use commercially published textbooks as reference materials. Some private publishers and social organizations, including the Nepalese Society for Children's Literature, are publishing children's books, but the country depends largely on book imports.

India is second only to the United States and the United Kingdom in the production of English-language books and has a vigorous publishing industry in seventeen other languages. The education system that must be supplied with learning materials is massive' 227 universities, 9,278 colleges, 98,134 high schools, 171,216 middle schools and 590,421 primary schools. Enrolment at the primary level alone is 100 million.

A process of devolution from the central government to the states is almost complete. Under it, the state governments will produce nearly all the textbooks, work books and teachers' guides for primary schools and the majority of textbooks for secondary and senior secondary schools. The goal is to provide the books at an affordable price, which the private sector has failed to do. Private schools draw on both locally produced and imported books. Tertiary-level texts are for the most part published locally, but postgraduate and research needs are met mainly by importation.In India the Rajiv Gandhi Foundation is building networks of village libraries and stocking them with books and newspapers in the local language. The libraries are run by village committees that are responsible for providing suitable premises for the library, identifying a librarian, and general financial management. They are expected to become financially self-sustaining through low membership fees, municipal grants, and donations. The foundation supplies initial financing, furniture, training for the librarian and a collection of about 400 books, chosen with community assistance. Efforts are made to integrate the collection with other local rural development projects. Books are lent among libraries to obtain diversity at minimum cost. The libraries are intended to lend books for reading at home. There is not enough accommodation in most villages for reading rooms and there is concern that women might hesitate to use a reading room that becomes a place where men congregate.

In Maldives the only bookstores are in the capital, Malé, and transportation between the islands is poor. None the less, the overall literacy rate is 98.8 per cent, and 99.3 per cent for females. Book production is expensive as a result of the small market and dependence on imported materials. Textbooks are produced and subsidized by the government. There is a serious shortage of learning materials in the local languages. There are few local writers, especially in the national language, Dhivehi, and to encourage them the government holds writing competitions, including some for children's literature. Most of the libraries are concentrated in Malé but some atolls have school libraries and community reading centres.

In Pakistan textbooks have long been produced by the four provincial textbook boards, but the market has recently been opened to competition from private sources. Other categories of learning materials have been neglected. There is a shortage of school and public libraries, and an imbalance between educational and general publishing: textbooks account for some 70 per cent of the total book production. Special efforts are being made, with the UNESCO office in Pakistan, to educate the children of refugees from Afghanistan, where the education system is in disarray.

The Sri Lankan government is responsible for supplying free textbooks for Grades 1 to 11, but does so in collaboration with the private sector. Some thirty-five commercial publishing houses are active as well as the state's Educational Publications Department. The National Book Development Council is a permanent body attached to the Ministry of Education and Higher Education and the industry enjoys an'approved undertaking' status that secures for it special benefits. A World Bank/International Development Association book development project, just under way, includes the rewriting of some 220 textbooks, the establishment of 2,000 new school libraries and the improvement of 1,000 existing ones, and the training of authors, illustrators, book designers, librarians and other personnel.

Broadcasting

Three main types of broadcasting used for primary and junior secondary school children – direct teaching, school broadcasting designed as enrichment and general children's programming. In practice, as we have seen, there can be a blurring of edges between them. Together, however, they can create a loose but formidable mosaic of learning opportunities for this group of learners. Interactive radio is the best documented. It has been pioneered and developed mainly by the United States Agency for International Development (USAID) from the 1970s up to the present day in over twenty Latin American, African and Asian countries. With assistance from UNESCO, the Netherlands government and USAID, these countries are involved, in the joint development of IRI curriculum materials in mathematics and Portuguese as a second language.During the twenty-five years of IRI projects, a significant research base has grown out of project evaluations and these can help us gain insight into conditions for success and sustainability for radio teaching projects. There is consistent evidence of learning gains among children who have followed IRI lessons. But some problems remain. One is that of scale and cost.

The achievements of interactive radio have to be set against the relatively high cost of the curriculum development on which they are based. In a significant number of cases, IRI has proved not to be sustainable beyond a pilot stage because Ministries of Education could not meet the costs. Operation at a pilot scale is likely to keep unit costs relatively high. There may be conflict between the demands of scale – seeking to maximize audience and keep materials in use as long as possible – and the needs to be responsive to local needs and shifting needs in learning. Materials with long-production lead times (and from the cost point of view a long shelf-life) cannot easily be responsive in these ways.

Broadcasting is particularly susceptible to the promise that all that is lacking in an impoverished and limited education system is an adequate means for depositing ready- made education; that adaptations of projects from one culture to another are straightforward. In practice IRI cannot be expected – nor was designed – to transform education systems. Successive evaluations of educational broadcasting generally show that it is likely to succeed if it grows out of prevailing pedagogical practices, and community, professional and national networks through a process of continuous research and dialogue. IRI is therefore likely to have limited success if it is seen as being imposed externally. In South Africa, for example, the original plans for an IRI project were rejected on grounds that their apparently behaviourist pedagogy was dangerously close to prescriptive, teacher-centred aspects of apartheid education. Only when it was reshaped on constructivist premises was it acceptable. IRI continues to be faced by a concern that it may reduce, even usurp, a teacher's control and responsibilities. In addressing that concern, too, it needs to explore how to broaden the concept of interactivity away from a simulated conversation and overcome the top-down, one-way nature of radio. During the 1990s IRI has developed initiatives in heath education and early childhood development that attempt to answer some of these questions.

Using a 'decentralized implementation methodology', preventive health and education programmes are marketed and disseminated on cassette to local radios and local municipalities and, through decentralized training, adapted culturally for different language groups. However, this sort of decentralized system involves higher costs, is more time-consuming and labour intensive. While we have much less documentation on other uses of radio, there is some evidence that fills out this picture of radio's strength and weakness in formal education. Flavell and Micallef, for example, working in Mozambique, attempted to measure the relative effectiveness of a radio-only approach and a radio-plus approach (teaching materials and teaching assistance) in terms of improvement in English language skills among students at a secondary level. Following large-scale longitudinal sampling over a nine-month period in seven Mozambican state schools, they concluded that general exposure to radio is beneficial but markedly so when radio is used in conjunction with good quality local print materials and where local teachers are well trained in the use of radio and audio-cassettes in class.

Used in this more integrated way, radio can be exploited in a far greater range of educational strategies and with greater effect than a radio-only approach. Studies from the BBC English project, called Radio English Direct, which is taking place in a number of African countries, are also likely to prove useful. Radio programmes and materials are being developed within particular countries that reflect teachers' and students' concerns, and existing educational conditions and curricula. Part of the project has been the development of a radio awareness element within the teacher-training curriculum. More studies are required to measure the effectiveness of radio in formal education. An innovative new direction in schools broadcasting is child-or teacher-initiated schools broadcasting at the local level. As already mentioned the Kothmale radio station in Sri Lanka serves remote rural communities and receives from children or their teachers' requests for further information about school topics for which no local resources exist. The producers search the Internet for resources, download them and then construct programmes around the information or release it in printed form back to the school or at the station' public access centre. This directly responsive relationship between school and broadcasters overcomes, to a large degree, the one-way, top-down nature of much broadcasting and perhaps points to a future area of development. There are also examples of television school broadcasting based, as in rich countries, within large broadcasting corporations and as part of television channels. In developing countries these tend to the product of the Ministry of Education and Ministry of Information or Curriculum Development Centres. We distinguished above between formal and non-formal children's programming.

International experience provides a number of examples of projects that use a non-formal approach and may allow use either in school or outside. Some programmes are designed with the content of the school curriculum in mind. Colombia's Ricon del Cuento programme, for example, is a forty-seven-part television series for 4-to-8-year-olds, designed to promote a love of reading. It has been broadcast on public television and also distributed to 1,500 schools in Colombia on cassettes. The British Broadcasting Corporation's hugely successful factual documentary, Walking with Dinosaurs, is broadcast at peak family viewing times in the evenings but has generated a range of learning resources in and out of school such as books bought commercially, and on-line resources for teachers and young learners. In South Africa, in a move further away from the conventional curriculum, the South Africa Broadcasting Corporation produce Lifeskills print packages for schools, based on the characters and stories in its prime time Soul City television and radio series, and produced in nine languages. These schools' activities are just one element within a broader campaign that creates a whole mosaic of mutually reinforcing educational opportunities.There has also been a growth in children-driven or child-centred programmes. This trend is a particularly noticeable in programmes with a conflict-resolution curriculum.

There is a renaissance in the use of radio and television broadcasting as teaching tools for both formal and non-formal purposes. The widespread ownership of both makes this an obvious development. At present there is more emphasis on radio in developing countries but some are arguing that television for learning will become a foremost tool in the twenty-first century. A critical mass of TV viable countries now exists for educational purposes, to justify unprecedented levels of international co-ordination in such areas as experience exchange, training, resource development, and national and regional capacity building.

Expansion of secondary schooling is constrained by a shortage of qualified teachers, particularly in rural areas, and a shortage of school buildings. Inevitably, secondary experience has lagged behind primary. Coverage in urban areas is much higher than elsewhere but still remains insufficient while adolescents in low-density rural areas present a particular problem: schooling is often unfeasible due to low student numbers, the difficulty of attracting and retaining teachers, and the difficulty of offering a range of specialist courses. Gender, ethnic back-ground, class and caste, as well as location, affect children's chances of getting to secondary school. Various technology-enhanced initiatives have been used to address needs of the out-of-school children and adolescents. These can be grouped into three categories: first, those that offer direct teaching in alternative secondary systems; second, smaller-scale, non-formal, outreach learning opportunities; and third, resource-based self-access learning opportunities.

In rich countries computer-based virtual classrooms have been developed for out-of-school adolescents. The majority of these, as we have seen earlier, are focused on individual subject areas and used by in-school learners as additional resources. The John D. Bracco School in Alberta, Canada, has taken this a step further and is operating as a dual-mode school: in parallel to its mainstream schooling curriculum, it offers a full alternative junior high school programme – LearnNet – for adolescents in remote areas or parents who wish to educate their children at home. LearnNet gives guidance from professional educators to home-schooled students and their parents through a computer conferencing system, although students may occasionally come to the school to socialize, to meet their teachers and to attend classes. The Rocky View Virtual School offered a full course load to over 185 students in Grades 9-12 in 1998/99 and expanded to include Grades 7 and 8 in 1999/00. Course are offered in a wide range of subjects in three different streams – the academic route required for university entrance, the non-academic route required for college entrance and the lower academic route for students looking towards an apprenticeship after graduation.

Television-based schools are exemplified by Mexico's Telesecundaria programme which has been providing direct television teaching to increasing numbers of rurally based learners. Centrally produced television programmes covering the same secondary school curriculum as that offered in ordinary schools are beamed via satellite throughout the country on a scheduled daily basis to Telesecundaria schools in two shifts. Each hour focuses on a different subject area and typically follows the same routine – fifteen minutes of television, switch-off, and then book-led and teacher-led activities. Different levels in the same subject are staggered to begin at exactly the point at which the preceding level switches off. The child is exposed to a variety of teachers on television but has one home teacher at the school for all disciplines in each grade. Some 60 per cent of Telesecundaria teachers are fully qualified while 40 per cent are university graduates with no previous teacher training. They receive induction training and then follow-up in-service training through televised programmes broadcast in the afternoons or on

Saturdays. Following the introduction of satellite transmission, the numbers of learners grew from 512,700 in 1993 to 817,200 by the end of 1997/98, with a projected enrolment of 1,100,000 by 2004.

Radio has advantages over television, in terms of access as well as cost, for countries with a low population density. Mongolia provides an example. The change to an open market economy created new challenges for the Mongolian education system in order to cater for new demands of basic education, retraining, continuing education and literacy training for both young people and adults. With over a third of the population living a nomadic life with an economy based on animal husbandry, radio-centred distance education has become widely used in Mongolia for this and other levels. Learning for Life, a UNESCO and Mongolian government programme launched in 1997, is to target marginalized youth throughout the country over a four-year period. This amounts to 37,000 selected families who, through radio programmes, self-learning booklets, learning centres, teacher-training sessions, acquire competencies in micro-enterprises and marketing. Open Schools represent a different approach to out of school education.

In response to an unmet demand for places at secondary level, the central governments of India, Indonesia and the Republic of Korea have created alternative systems for young learners unable to get into mainstream schools. This Asian model of open schools, though differing in certain particulars, is distinctive because it retains close connections with the regular secondary school system. Students learn from self-instructional materials used in conjunction with different combinations of low-tech cassettes and broadcasts and differing types of student's support. The National Open

School, India oversees the development of self-instructional print and sometimes audiocassette materials by other educational institutions including mainstream schools, the National Council for Educational Research and Training (NCERT) and the Indira Gandhi National Open University. They offer four different types of programmes in English and Hindi: secondary, senior-secondary (Grades 10-12), bridge courses (around Grade 8) and vocational courses (free-standing or combined with academic courses). A student in the secondary level can choose home science and business studies, in addition to mathematics, science, English, social studies, or bakery and confectionery. At the senior-secondary level, a student may choose subjects, such as political science, chemistry, or furniture and cabinet making. There are no formal entry requirements for the programmes, and the range of courses and the freedom to select is often better than in many schools.

With its capacity to reach large numbers of adults even in remote locations, broadcasting has been widely used for adult education. Attempts have been made to provide learner support, based on existing social networks and linked with broadcasts. Participatory approaches have driven a shift towards public-interest broadcasting with programmes planned around identified audience needs and requests. There is a long history of projects that seek to link group study and activity with broadcasts. Radio listening groups – also known as listening forums and clubs – make use of local educational broadcasts addressed to groups of learners who meet with a community teacher on a regular basis. Group discussions precede and follow the broadcasts, and are often accompanied by additional flipchart material demonstrated by the teacher. The broadcasts usually centre on health and agricultural issues, and may include related literacy work. The community teacher provides feedback – and sometimes actual recordings – to the radio broadcasters who then incorporate them into their future broadcasts. Video forums are similar in set-up.

Many non-governmental organizations in Peru are involved in the production of alternative videos for development work among a wide range of beneficiaries. The videos, which centre on journalist analyses of urban and rural issues from fifteen different, mainly Latin America countries, are produced by development video specialists working in dedicated audio-visual and teaching aid centres.

The objectives of such centres are 'education, dissemination of innovations, social promotion and participation within marginalised urban sectors and in the campesino communities'. High production values and audience research have gone into preferred audiovisual formats; for example, it was found that documentaries and narrative reports are preferred over fiction. Most video forum work is done in Lima, the provinces and the southern part of the country, with the main beneficiaries being women and district community groups.

Half-hour videos are shown one to two times a week, with an average of forty viewers per showing. The forum around the video lasts for about an hour.Small-scale, community radio stations can directly interact with the audience they serve. In remote or isolated areas they can operate in a multifunctional way, providing the means for accessing a wide variety of vocational, business, health and agricultural information.

Computers

Computers have been used in an attempt to change, strengthen and improve basic education in a variety of different ways and for a variety of different purposes. We start by looking at the rationales for using computers in education and then at strategies for making them available to learners. It is worth distinguishing between various different rationales for using computers in education so that policy decisions can sensibly reflect educational purpose. An analysis by the Commonwealth Secretariat, which drew on reviews of Commonwealth-wide practice, usefully distinguished four rationales for introducing computers to education; the development of Internet communications means that we now need to add a fifth.

1 To build a resource of people who are highly skilled in the use of information technology. Where governments see information technology as a means of strengthening the economy, and want to develop a workforce with vocational skills for computer-related activities, computer-education programmes have been set up to develop a cadre of people with specialist skills.

2. To equip all students for a future in which technological awareness and basic computer skills will increasingly be important for greater numbers of citizens. Countries have adopted this approach as they see that, whether or not the country is likely to be a producer of computer hardware or software, their citizens need to be in a strong position to take advantage of technological developments as they arise.

3. To use the technology to enhance the existing curriculum and to improve the way in which it is developed. Computer-assisted learning programs, in which the computer takes over some of the activity of the teacher, fall within this rationale.

4. To promote change in education by moving towards a more relevant curriculum and a new definition of the teacher's role. Some computer projects have been designed to shift the curriculum in the direction of practical learning of information-handling and communication skills rather than concentration on memory.

5. To allow learners to seek information from databases, especially through the Internet, and use computer technology to communicate with other schools, colleges and learning communities. This rationale opens up new learner-initiated opportunities.

The rationales overlap and national policies may embrace more than one but their curricular and cost implications are different. The first rationale leads to investment in courses at the upper end of secondary education, in vocational training and in tertiary education. Whole-hearted adoption of the second rationale, concerning the education of all future citizens, suggests that computer-related education should be at the upper end of the universal stage of education. It is likely, too, that educational content will rely on generic software – allowing children to develop basic skills in wordprocessing or the use of databases and spreadsheets for example – rather than the use of subject-specific computer-aided learning. The third rationale has been the subject of the most severe criticism; early computer-aided learning proved to have high unit costs and, in many cases, simply offered an expensive way of offering drill and practice, with keyboard and mouse instead of pen and paper. The fourth and fifth rationales both suggest that, if computers are to be used in school, it is necessary to think through their consequences for the curriculum; changes in the curriculum will not occur through technology alone. The fifth rationale presents new opportunities for reshaping the curriculum but demands not only that schools should have access to computers, but also have, and can pay for, access to the Internet. No matter which rationale dominates, the use of computers in the classroom presents significant demands to ministries of education. Computer equipment – hardware – needs to be provided and accompanied by appropriate software. Staff using computers need training.

Where computers are used mainly, or even partly, for access to the Internet, then reliable telephone access and an agreement with an Internet service provider are also required. We look at the costs involved below and turn next to the strategic issues involved in getting access to computer technologies for schools, and in some cases for getting access to the Internet.

Use of information and communication technologies in education has been constrained by economics. At present, few low-or middle-income countries have been able to develop nationwide programmes for the use of computers in the classroom. Where there are programmes to develop educational capacity in information and communication technology, they tend either to concentrate on tertiary education or to be limited to a small number of, usually, urban, schools in a pilot project. These initiatives may form the first stages in an overall government strategy or be piecemeal developments dictated by budgetary limitations, political interest and serendipity. Throughout the world, there is a clear pecking order when integrating communication technologies into the formal educational system – tertiary downwards and with primary education low on the list. This situation is changing mainly in Organisation for Economic Co-operation and Development (OECD) countries and newly industrialized countries (NIC) for various reasons: national communications policies; increased governmental funding; the integration of the technologies into all levels of national curricula; generally far cheaper hardware and software and increased private ownership. These governments are now funding nationwide initiatives to build up hardware, software and accompanying skills at all educational levels, including the lower secondary, primary and even nursery levels. As a result, various different approaches have been adopted to enable schools to get access to computer hardware and software.

Internet

Improved telecommunications may have implications far beyond formal schooling of the kind which has dominated our discussion so far. We look below at the significance of improved communications in health and medicine, with potential benefits for health education. Telecommunications have, for example, the potential to help countries with limited medical expertise and resources. Telemedicine and telehealth are health delivery systems that increase the medical and health resources available to medical practitioners for diagnosis and treatment between two or more locations using technology-assisted communications. The technology can vary between basic telephony, digital land line, cellular/ wireless, satellite and broadband networks such as ATM.

Telemedicine services include access to remote expert systems (teleconsultations) and remote sensing (telecardiology, telepathology and teleradiology). It is suitable for long-distance, emergency patient treatment in areas without a sophisticated health service such as at sea and in remote or war-torn areas. The consultations, for example, can take place in real time by radio, telephone or videoconferencing or off-line via e-mail exchanges. Telehealth, more the domain of health workers, is to do with preventative health care or the provision of health services to those who are at a distance from the service providers but who are not necessarily ill. This includes access to remote national or international telehealth resources concerning the prevention and identification of serious diseases documentation centres, databanks, information networks, electronic conferences, on-line medical journals and courses. Databank examples include INFOLEP, MEDLINE, AVLINE, BIOETHICLINE and TOXLINE. Documentation centres include CANCERLIT and web versions of leading medical journals such as Lancet.

The Internet, specialist software and CD-ROMs are increasingly used in rich country contexts and in a range of different educational settings, including supplementary schooling for refugees, Hebrew and Muslim special schools, in remote areas and community centres. The Internet is typically used to establish new national or international learning networks between groups of children in school or community centres. Examples include Inuit schools in the Northwest Territories of the Arctic and Jewish schools throughout the diaspora. It is also used, by children or their teachers, to access new or specialist learning resources. The latter are frequently posted on dedicated websites that provide information, contacts, educational advice and ready-made materials for particular minority or marginalized groups. Examples include the WEB DuBois Center for Afro-Americans, the Artemis Gypsy and Traveller Education Database, The Kids' Hospital Network, the Efecot and Pavee Point websites for travellers and the website of the Office of the United Nations High Commissioner for Refugees. Other projects are feeding into the creation of appropriate content: some fund the digitization of ethnic minority literature while others, like one initiated by the government of Tamil Nadu, promote keyboard standardization and software interfaces in different languages, such as Tamil. Software for language development is a particular growth area.

Providing education for travellers' children has produced innovative uses of technology. In the United States, for example, the Department of Education is providing some secondary-level learners with laptop computers that enable them to study online courses provided by a private education company. The FLEX project, involving twenty-three European–wide partners and with a budget of some 1.5 million euros (about $1,530,000), is exploring way of using the latest technologies to improve the education of travelling children (e.g. circus, fair-ground and bargee children). Travelling children are provided with laptop computers, CD-ROM learning resources, GSM modem and a digital video-broadcast receiver.

The school-based teacher sends messages and structured 'learning blocks' via a video-mail message. The child communicates with a remote tutor by leaving voice mail messages on the FLEX website. Another European project, TOPILOT, combines learning resources on a CD-I (interactive Compact Disc) and other print-based materials with cheap narrow-band mobile data-communication (via GSM). The tutor can monitor their learners' progress through the CD-I material from a distance. The examples here all concern marginalized children in rich countries. They have had to overcome the problems of geographical or cultural remoteness within a single country: even within national boundaries there can be differences between the information rich and the information poor. Remote communities are likely to have lower quality and less reliable communication links, sometimes at higher costs than those in urban centres.

4

Challenges of Technical and Vocational Education

Vocational education is strongly rooted in educational ideals and objectives, on the one hand, and is thoroughly permeated by labour market criteria and work standards, on the other. To ensure both the human and professional aspects of vocational education, two major dimensions should always guide the design of the relevant schemes and systems: education and work. The educational dimension caters more for the individual needs and human aspects, while the work or economic dimension caters more for societal needs and labour market requirements. Furthermore, modern approaches take it for granted that vocational education schemes and programmes cannot be designed to correspond accurately to a particular job.

The dynamics and changing demand of the labour market require more and more the replacement of physical skills by mental skills, and hence that such schemes and programmes be liberalised and broad-based, to promote adaptability, widen the scope of job opportunities, and enhance educational and occupational mobility.

One of the major challenges that is still encountered by policy makers and planners of vocational education systems, in developing as well as developed countries, is the ability to operationalize the concept of integration, rather than just that of co-ordination and coexistence, of educational and work values and standards, and hence the integration of individual and societal needs, interests and objectives. The schism or separation between the education system and the world of work, which is found in particular in most developing countries, is one of the major weaknesses of vocational education systems in these countries.

In many countries, especially industrialised ones, the centre of gravity of vocational education systems is generally located nearer to societal and labour market needs, at the expense of educational values and individual needs. In many other countries, especially developing ones, the centre of gravity is located nearer to educational criteria and standards, at the expense of labour market needs and employment requirements. There are three main vocational education issues will be explored, that are of special importance in general, and in developing countries in particular. These issues are:

— the economics of vocational education,

— the social status of vocational education, and

— the regional and international dimensions of vocational education.

The economics of vocational education is concerned with the sources of finance and methods of funding; while the second factor is concerned with such matters as costs, efficiency and effectiveness, and hence with the socio-economic return on investment in vocational education.

The sources of finance and methods of funding of vocational education programmes vary considerably. Nevertheless, two such sources predominate: the first represents the taxpayers through central and/or local budgets, while the second source represents employers in industry and business, who are the main beneficiaries of the output of vocational education systems.

Other sources with less impact include learners and trainees themselves and their families, in the case of fee-paying programmes; income generating activities; grants and donations, especially for such programmes as those directed to special groups, including the handicapped and the underprivileged. In most developing countries, public sources of finance for vocational education usually predominate. Public funding is in general utilised to finance school systems, and suffers usually from being inadequate, especially in countries with limited resources, where vocational education is not considered a priority in national budgets.

A dynamic multifaceted approach to the funding issue, with the objective of diversifying sources of finance, should be adopted in developing countries to ensure adequacy and sustainability of funding. Such an approach has yet to gain recognition and feasibility in such countries. Matters related to cost, efficiency and effectiveness of vocational education schemes, which represent the second factor concerning the economics of such schemes, pose a big challenge in most developing countries.

The relevant issues here include, on the planning or macro level, system choice or the school vs the enterprise issue, the broad vs. the narrow base approach to the area of specialisation, and the duration of the vocational education programme. On the operational or micro level, such issues include trainee-instructor ratios, utilisation factors of training facilities, choice of equipment and technologies, and size and nature of productive activities.

The economics of vocational education, are far from being common practice in developing countries. To be effective, evaluation systems should incorporate three main elements. The first is internal evaluation, which is mainly concerned with assessing the degree of compatibility between the outputs of the vocational education programme and the performance objectives specified for such programmes. The second element is the economic evaluation, which is basically concerned with such indicators as cost-benefit criteria, changes in learner's income, changes in productivity at the work place, comparative costing of different vocational education systems, and optimum utilisation of training facilities and services. The third element is external evaluation, which is generally concerned with assessing the degree of computability between the outputs of the vocational education programmes on the one hand, and labour market needs and employment requirements, on the other.

In developing countries, all aspects related to the economics of vocational education are sources of concern, and even frustration, especially when taking into consideration the relatively high cost of vocational education programmes, compared with other educational offerings.

The social status of vocational education in any society is, to a great extent, a reflection of the status of work values in that society. Traditional cultures and philosophies range between two extremes regarding their assessment of work values. At one extreme, the ancient Greek culture viewed work as a low-grade life activity that, nevertheless, can't be dispensed with; while at the other extreme, the Marxist culture viewed work as the supreme value. Between these two extremes, different cultures vary to some extent in their assessment of work values. A rational and balanced approach can be realised if work activities are assessed both by their material and economic returns on the individual and society, on the one hand; and their social and humanising influences, on the other.

Thus, vocational education systems and schemes should be designed as developmental life experiences that have their own social dimension and cultural extension. Vocational education, should do more than provide the learner with the specific skills and knowledge needed for the job. It should be acknowledged that occupations are more effectively performed by workers who are generally, as well as specifically prepared, taking into consideration the ongoing transformation of work processes, technologies and environments. The social status of vocational education can, on the other hand, be enhanced in practice through appropriate career guidance and counselling services, as well as employment and placement services.

Unfortunately, these two types of services are weak in most developing countries, accentuating more the status issues of vocational education. When such services exist, fully or partially, in developing or developed countries, it is not unusual for the providers of such services to fall in the trap of being guided more by labour market needs and employment priorities, than by the fulfilment of the individual's needs and inclinations, and the realisation of his potentialities.

Proper career guidance and employment services should fulfil both labour market and individual needs, and should not end up by adjusting or even distorting the learner's inclinations to labour market requirements. In practice, the social status of vocational education is also influenced, to a great extent, by the type of relation and nature of channels that link it with higher education that leads to the preparation of professionals.

Successful vocational education schemes are usually designed with inherent and built-in links with higher educational and occupational levels, through the formal or non-formal systems of education, within the general concept of continuing and life-long education. In some education systems, especially those of developing countries, the realisation of this concept would necessitate the restructuring and reform of higher education, in order to eliminate bottlenecks, and establish lateral and vertical channels among the various fields and levels of educational and training offerings, to promote occupational and educational mobility and, consequently social mobility.

In general, therefore, higher education should be linked with the abilities and performance standards of the learner, irrespective of the type or stream of pre-university education or training he/she experienced. Furthermore, the status of vocational education can be enhanced in practice through the establishment of a comprehensive and diversified network of non-formal and adult educational and training facilities and services which are accessible to the employed, as well as to the unemployed, to enable them move along and up the educational and professional ladder at any point or stage of their careers; thus fostering their personal development, enhancing their occupational and social mobility, and upgrading the quality and productivity of work sites.

In most developing countries, such facilities and services suffer from two main shortcomings. First, they fall short of the minimum requirements needed to have an impact in such aspects as quantity, quality, geographical coverage, flexibility and accessibility. Secondly, such facilities and services seem to be utilised more by those who are already better educated and who can afford the costs involved. Thus, instead of acting as a means to compensate for earlier inequalities in educational and training opportunities, and as a vehicle to contribute to bridging the social and economic gap between the various groups of society, adult education facilities and services face the risk, in most developing countries, of widening the educational, occupational and social gap between the privileged and the underprivileged, between the haves and the have-nots.

Other aspects of the status issue of vocational education include such factors as the status of the vocational teacher, the gender issue, and the vocationalization of general education. It is not unusual in many education and training systems to find that vocational teachers are not of equal status, socially and economically, to their general education counterparts. It is also not unusual to find that the relevant vocational education facilities and services are structured basically around the needs of male learners, with the result that the role of females as learners, instructors, planners and providers of services, lags considerably behind the role of males.

Finally, a great service can be offered to the status issue, if a strong element of vocational education, or more specifically prevocational education, is incorporated as part of general education in the form diversified practical activities and life experiences, derived from the various socio-economic sectors.

The regional and international dimensions of vocational education is related to human resources development in general, and vocational education in particular, is no more a purely national concern. For sometime now, it has been a regional concern; and now it is even becoming a concern with international dimensions that should take into consideration emerging conditions of increasingly globalized economies of the world, manifested by the changing structure and framework of world trade, labour mobility, common markets, commodity standards, multinationals, and the geographical characteristics of industrialisation.

The economies of developed Western countries, as an example, are shifting away from the manufacturing sector to the services sector, with much of the manufacturing activities moving to less developed countries in Asia and Latin America, attracted by reduced production costs. It is thus becoming increasingly essential to think regionally and even globally when planning, defining policies and designing programmes at the national level, for the quantitative and qualitative aspects of vocational education as a component of human resources development, especially in such matters as job classification, skill standards, educational levels, information systems and the identification of training needs.

There are two examples of the concepts of vocational education and vocational training. We frequently come across, or use, these two terms, sometimes to mean different things and sometimes to mean the same thing. The split and schism between Vocational Education and Vocational Training is believed to be artificial in modern vocational schemes and programmes. The fact that the split still exists is due probably to past prejudices and administrative structures.

The split might have been justified decades ago when it was usual for workers to acquire the skills needed for their jobs purely through traditional timeserving informal apprenticeship schemes, consisting predominantly of on-the-job practical experiences. This is no more the case now. Jobs are classified according to two main variables: the field of specialisation and the occupational level. The content of any vocational preparation programme for a job is analysed into its constituent functions, duties and skills, specifying the theoretical content and knowledge needed. Thus the needs and requirements of the job dictate the structure and content of the vocational programme, whether it is called vocational education or vocational training. The fact that the vocational programme is implemented in an educational institution or within a work environment in an enterprise should not affect the basic structure and content of the programme, simply because the needs and requirements of the job are independent of the venue that is utilised for the implementation of the preparation programme.

The schism between Vocational Education and Vocational Training can be ended, and the barriers demolished if vocational programmes are structured around the needs of the job and the needs of the learner, irrespective of the venue of implementation, or the agency responsible for its financing or administration. The two most renowned international agencies in the field of vocational education and training, UNESCO and ILO, need to address this issue seriously, so that we stop talking different things about what should be the same thing, and stop insisting that UNESCO's role is vocational education, while ILO's role is vocational training.

This is not role splitting, but rather hair splitting! It is worthwhile mentioning here in this context that, because UNESCO and ILO communicate with member countries through different channels and national agencies, two systems of human power preparation at the basic occupational levels emerge sometimes side by side with little or no co-ordination, and sometimes with rivalry and mistrust.

The regional and global dimensions of vocational education cannot be properly explored without investigating their cultural reflections and outreaches, especially that globalisation is a trend that is permeating all aspects of life: economic, social and cultural. This would obviously present another challenge to planners of vocational education systems, and would justify more the broad-based human approach to vocational education programmes to complement the professional and specialised approach.

In China, on the eve of the 21st century, however, building walls will definitely not be an adequate response to the challenges we face in education. There are three pivotal developments of the past 20 years that have caused most of the change:

— microprocessor technology and its impact on information, communication, production, and work organisation; biotechnology and genetic technology;

— the end of the cold war and the division of the world into blocs of capitalism and communism; and

— growing ecological consciousness.

Information technology (IT) is at the root of a process of transformation in the course of which industrialised societies are changing into knowledge societies and the management of production into the management of knowledge. There will be less and less manual work while computers become the main tools catering for the information needs of all professions. The end of the division of the world has opened the borders to the free flow of capital, goods and information and to the unhindered travel of people at large, but not yet in all parts of the world. Going global is the challenge to entrepreneurs and, of course, to their employees.

As an example, cross-border activities in a united Europe demand the same competencies in all participating countries, i.e. language and more knowledge about partner countries, their economy, culture and their legal and social systems. Growing ecological consciousness will become a very important economic factor in the foreseeable future.

Eco-knowledge is an important part of it, but eco-thinking is even more important. It has to be part of all education, general and vocational. Curriculum revisions, new syllabuses or educational reforms cannot master all these changes. There is a point in this development where a new balance in responsibility in the partnership between management and the workforce now tilts more towards the workforce than prevailed in the past. This is not the result of a power struggle but the consequence of inevitable changes in the organisation of work.

In several European countries these changes are also reflected in government policies and ultimately in what is expected of VET. Tripartite bodies are responsible for VET-Standard development and implementation in many countries of the world. Thus, the ability of employers and trade unions to describe rather exactly what their needs are concerning the role and the competence profile of future skilled workers and employees has been developed and improved.

The communication between the world of work and the world of education, which very often seems to be nonexistent, has grown into a new culture within research institutes or employment offices where these tripartite bodies meet regularly. One of the most dangerous consequences of fundamental changes now prevailing in politics and, of course, in education is uncertainty and following this - anxiety.

In Eastern Europe, where nearly all established frameworks and structures have fallen apart, uncertainty and anxiety are probably the prime reasons for the failure of leadership, but also in western industrialised countries on their way into knowledge societies, some of them with particularly high unemployment rates, as well as in Asian countries which are shaken by a threatening economic crisis or in Africa and South-America uncertainty and anxiety are well known companions for a majority of people.

Therefore, it is one of the most important tasks of education to enable people to cope successfully with uncertainty through:

- — information and knowledge about the reasons for the changes, including systems' knowledge (e.g. computer systems, banking systems, free-market systems);
- — skills on how to gather and select information and knowledge, and how to use them in planning and decision-making processes;
- — problem-solving and practical skills, social and team skills;
- — entrepreneurial skills; and
- — The development of the learner's personality through general, vocational and professional education.

If education shall act successfully in this very important field, educators need the help of the whole society, not only parents. The corporate world and the trade unions have a responsibility for co-operation with the world of education for their own sake. A main task of education, including vocational education and training, must surely be to maintain the freedom to hold diverse opinions regardless of political, religious and philosophical boundaries. In the information driven world of work:

- — computers are the common tool for managers as well as for front line workers;
- — all information is being digitised and transformed into computer-compatible letters and figures;
- — the Internet is established as a worldwide information web, using English as the lingua franca of the knowledge age.

Initial vocational education and training pursue in their turn the kind of educational objectives that have traditionally been the prerogative of general education. They include:

- — learning to learn (on the job; integrating theory with practice; learning by reviewing practice; applying learning methods in practice; developing social capabilities that cannot be taught); and
- — becoming a mature and responsible contributor (acquiring overarching capabilities like acting in a group, thinking in process terms, taking responsibility for others and for one's own achievement).

The traditional boundaries between general and vocational education on the one hand and education and training on the other have become obstacles to learning for real life. There is no one-way-road of learning transfer from the so-called industrialised countries to the so-called developing world. Those who believe that they already know the problems of tomorrow have already lost the learning competition.

Education should also enable them to earn their own living and take part in the democratic process. All educational systems have to serve these purposes. Vocational education, i.e. the education and training of skilled workers and employees, has to be broader and more diversified. For example:

- — a car mechanic must have diagnostic skills and knowledge (computer literacy), be customer oriented (direct personal contact), have all the skills of the trade (high tech), must take into account the ecological effects of his/her work, be able to calculate the cost of a repair and, more generally, be conscious of adding value;

— a farmer or horticulturist must be knowledgeable in biology, chemistry, management, marketing, engineering (mechanical) and have customer orientation; he/she must be able to find and exploit niches in the market (e.g. value added products for hotels in the neighbourhood);

— a worker in one of the growing service industries e.g. in the tourist, hospitality or leisure industry can be a well educated and trained leisure manager with a broad cultural background and communication skills; and

— a health care assistant in one of the broadest fields of services where people of all ages can perform full time or part-time services once they have access to adequate education and training.

Vocational education is to create learning opportunities through which people can develop their ability to learn autonomously and use what they have learned to make a difference in their workplace. In Germany, government, employers and trade unions agreed in 1987 that all occupational (VET)-standards should include the new overall objective which changed the former VET-paradigm. All new learning activities following this new paradigm have one characteristic incommon: the learner steps into the centre of the learning process, gathers information and, as far as possible, acts independently. The teacher/trainer also changes his/her role to become coach, advisor and tutor.

The changes in technology, business, politics and society, all make it necessary to re-examine the aims, contents, qualifications and methods of all educational systems. Will they help or hinder future developments? All over the world VET-standards are benchmarked, newly developed or revised. The setting of new educational standards is more than just another reform, it has become a movement.

The countries of Central and Eastern Europe and those that formed the former Soviet Union, the so-called "countries in transition" are confronted with the most radical change that educational systems have ever had to endure, especially in such a short time. With the change in the overall philosophy from centralised planning to free markets, these countries have to build new vocational education systems and transform all occupational and professional standards and curricula. This endeavour needs solidarity and support. The European Training Foundation (ETF) based in Turin, Italy was founded in 1994 to support the Central and Eastern European countries to restructure their vocational education and training (VET) systems.

ETF's Advisory Forum embraces the member states of the EU and the countries of the former Eastern Bloc and - as of 1999 - the Mediterranean countries of Africa and the Near East (MEDA-Programme 1999) as well as international institutions like CEDEFOP, the EU's VET-centre, UNESCO, ILO, the World Bank and European Employer and Trade Union Associations. The task of the Forum is to discuss the needs of the countries in transition in the field of VET and advise the ETF Directorate and its Governing Board by defining adequate measures of support in its programme planning.

The European Union is focussing on this very important factor in its vocational education promotion programmes in order to improve the data base for future oriented VET-planning processes, to better link learning in schools and at the workplace, to help teachers in coping with the large amount of new knowledge , new skills and new methods of teaching with the support of multimedia and setting new VET-standards. Vocational education research and development could also be a key to innovative measures to make better use of informal learning achievements for young and adult with little formal education.

The world is moving towards an information-based economy where the effectiveness of an enterprise or a country is determined by the quality of its products and services. Production systems based on new technologies that enable greater productivity and flexibility demand that all workers constantly must update their skills and become more entrepreneurial. The evidence clearly shows that the most productive nations are those characterised by a flexible and well-qualified labour market, one with a rich and diverse mix of skills which are continuously updated and developed throughout life.

Technical and vocational education and training (TVET) is most directly concerned with the acquisition of the knowledge and skills required for the world of work, formal and informal, urban and rural. And every country must adapt its TVET programme to cater to the skill requirements of its workplace of the twenty-first century. These skills requirements may vary considerably according to the stage of socio-economic development of each country.

Nevertheless, it has been clearly demonstrated that every country, regardless of its state of development, is compelled to redesign its national TVET programme if it is to address effectively the employment and development issues of the next century. The economic situation can change dramatically suddenly, creating massive problems of unemployment and forcing many young people to opt for self-employment in the future.

In today's interdependent world, it is undoubtedly in the interests of the industrialised countries to provide tangible support to the efforts being made by developing countries to develop their human resources and to break the vicious cycle of poverty, inequity, unemployment, violence. Unemployment is now an international problem, one which cannot be contained within national boundaries. The provision of technical and vocational education and training aiming to prepare qualified technicians and skilled and semiskilled workers should be an essential component of the development agenda of all countries.

TVET is a bridge to the future, but there must be an employment road to which it leads, otherwise we create further problems. Thus we need not just a revitalised and more coherent TVET programme, but a new vision for TVET and employment - we need new models of TVETE, linking education, training, employment and social welfare, nationally and internationally. UNESCO would like to call upon all international organisations with an interest in technical and vocational education and training to join the efforts in serving the needs of all countries, particularly the developing nations, in reforming their TVET systems.

In an era characterised by the challenge of globalisation, rapid technological changes and economic uncertainty, it is imperative that all stakeholders work together to develop legislation and policies, establish institutional structures and redesign curricula to ensure that TVET caters adequately to the varied needs of all members of society to enter and re-enter the world of work. For this purpose, continuous TVET opportunities should be provided for achieving both personal and social development. UNESCO's activities therefore should aim at:

— Including vocational subjects in general education curricula to facilitate the young generation to obtain generic technological knowledge and key pre-vocational skills - making TVET for all an integral part of national educational policy;

— Developing the articulation between technical and vocational education on the one hand, and other sectors of education on the other, emphasising the recognition of prior learning and work experience, and raising the status of TVET in education systems;

— Promoting co-ordination between formal education and informal training systems, ministries responsible for education, training, labour and social welfare;

— Fostering the involvement of all stakeholders, particularly private sectors, in the provision of TVETE and improving the link and co-operation with the world of work.

TVET can play an instrumental role in developing a new generation of individuals who will face the challenge of achieving sustainable socio-economic development. A number of new subjects (issues) therefore need to be incorporated into TVET teaching and learning or be further emphasised for the sake of the future of all of us as we struggle to learn throughout life. A well-trained technical workforce is essential for any country's efforts to achieve sustainable development. Thus, UNESCO's activities should aim at:

— Ensuring that TVET is an integral part of every nation's development agenda, and a valued and integral part of its education and human resource development strategy;

— Including environmental issues in all TVET curricula with the objective of promoting the concept of sustainable development;

— Emphasising the acquisition of entrepreneurial skills, creativity, team and communication skills as part of TVET;

— Introducing and applying the new information and communication technologies in the TVET teaching and learning process without losing valuable aspects of traditional teaching methods;

— Paying special attention to providing training for the tourism and hospitality industries which are a potential avenue towards employment creation and economic growth in the developing world.

TVET is also expected to be an instrument for social cohesion and integration. The general access to and availability of TVET and the right to work are closely inter-linked issues. Promoting special initiatives and efforts to ensure equal access to TVET for girls and women, and to eliminate the very strong historic gender basis against women which has for too long characterised TVET policy and practice.

Making TVET programmes, both formal and informal, available to the unemployed and various marginalised groups including early school leavers, the disabled, the rural poor, displaced persons and demobilised solders in post-conflict situations, contributing to the UN effort to alleviate poverty.

UNESCO will seek to forge an international alliance in support of TVET. The overall planning and monitoring of UNESCO's long term Programme on Technical and Vocational Education will be the responsibility of the Secretariat at UNESCO Headquarters, and will promote co-operation with other international partners. Particular attention will be paid to enhancing co-operation and promoting activities at regional and sub-regional levels. UNESCO, with the collaboration of ILO, will launch a one-stop website on the Internet dedicated to supporting TVET, to be known as the "TVET Implementation Centre". It will place online critical information and guidelines, examples of best practices, etc. with guided search and assist features, to cater for users of different levels in Member States. While UNESCO is the leading agency in the United Nations System in the field of education, many other intergovernmental and non-governmental agencies also deal with various aspects of education and training. In planning and implementing its Programme on Technical and Vocational Education, UNESCO will seek to develop close co-operation with other partners giving the Programme an interagency character.

Many countries find, TVE is costly and it difficult to sustain it without a continued supply of substantial resources. The popular notion that TVE should be demand driven does not consider the many situations especially in developing countries where such demand may not be present. The links between TVE and higher education are often weak and in some cases non-existent. This is a major discouragement to those bright students who would have liked to pursue their education and training to higher levels.

The need for TVE to be integrated in the national education system derives not only from its economic contribution but also from cultural, social and political needs. TVE should be viewed as a necessary activity and therefore an integral part of education accessible to all throughout life. Technological literacy and knowledge should be democratized and be made available to enable the beneficiaries to make the right choices about the use of technology.

New competencies and approaches are required: the need to learn continually about how to solve problems, the ability to cope with uncertainty, the ability to innovate and the ability to work with others are essential today and will increasingly be so in the future. There is a need for renewed popularization and support for TVE. This can be achieved through favourable policy initiatives, media support particularly through radio and television, and community support activities targeting the role of TVE development. There is still need for more concerted efforts at the international level to support TVE.

There is an urgent need to link up TVE with higher education to give opportunities to those beneficiaries of TVE who desire and have the capacity to pursue advanced studies and training. Due to the high cost of TVE the majority of those who could benefit from it do not have access. TVE programmes are often de-linked from the production process and to a large extent are delivered using traditional theoretical methods. TVE does not address the needs of the informal sector where most production activities go on. The assurance of quality programmes and the award of various forms of certification is another major challenge for TVE.

Partnerships between TVE institutions and enterprises will foster better working relationships that will support and strengthen TVE programmes. This will also give the TVE teachers and trainers opportunities to update their experiences. There is a need to find alternative methods of delivery of instruction for TVE. Teaching institutions and teachers should be reoriented to use flexible teaching and learning materials.

Some of these should include: the development of modularized curricula and assessment methods; the development and use of appropriate technologies for instruction - online services and training materials, computerized learning packages, use of CD-Roms, intranet and internet, etc. In order to ascertain the quality of programmes and the award of appropriate credentials, it is necessary to:

a) develop widely recognized qualification standards and use them for certification;

b) develop appropriate tools for assessing practical skills; and

c) have flexible and transferable qualifications.

Current TVE teacher training was identified as problematic because university staff need improved training themselves and industry experience. A framework for teacher training needs to be identified which recognises regional differences but which establishes high standards. Competencies required for teachers were agreed to include all areas of professional, general and social knowledge and skills, and that they are complex and changing frequently.

TVE teacher training needs to be given the same recognition as teachers in general and higher education and that TVE teacher training needs to be continuous/life long learning. A key reason for the drift of TVE teachers to industry was seen to be that they are not valued sufficiently, reflected in salary scales, and they can attract higher pay in industry and are therefore lost to TVE. Relationship with industry needs was discussed. A problem was identified as how industry demands can be balanced with the need to develop the whole individual through the provision of a general education component of TVE. Work experience for teachers was identified as a critical factor in providing TVE which has greater relevance.

Entrepreneurship education leads to a natural consequence of collaboration with workplaces and enterprises. Teachers need to have workplace knowledge and experience in order to teach students in this field of education. Entrepreneurship education was identified to include:

— External entrepreneurship—setting up as independent owner-entrepreneur;

— Internal entrepreneurship—includes work motivation, responsible flexibility, innovativeness, creativity and self-regulation i.e. personal responsiveness;

— Self directedness; and

— Entrepreneurship—can be incorporated into the educational policy goals at all levels.

TVE curriculum development encompassing environmental issues needs immediate attention since environmental concerns are urgent. Strategies may include the introduction of environmental issues and appropriate foreign languages into curriculum using an integrated approach to ensure that environmental issues are not treated as add-on courses.

Although governments carry the primary responsibility for TVE, in a modern market economy TVE policy design and delivery must be achieved through a new partnership between government, employers, vocations, industry, trades union and society. The role of the state will remain pivotal in creating the necessary enabling environment to enhance the participation of its social partners. This may be achieved through legislation, upgrading policy design and in delivery systems.

The state must be concerned principally with the creation of a policy framework for education and training that forms part of the national development plans for change. Together with its partners the state will facilitate, co-ordinate, regulate and monitor quality assurance across both the supply and the demand sides. These responsibilities must extend to public and private institutions; general education and TVE; formal, non-formal and informal education; rural and urban populations; with equal force to both genders; all age groups; the able and the disabled; and large, small and medium sized enterprises.

By employing such an approach the state and its social partners are more likely to build stronger economies, enhance social cohesion, humanity and the protection of the environment. It will also widen participation in education and training that will promote a culture of lifelong learning. The partnership between the state and the other stakeholders must work towards the ultimate objective of creating a learning society. A vibrant economy is best served by a diversity of public and private providers of TVE.

The combination or balance between the providers may be struck in many ways but the government should ensure strong basic preparation by all providers. Government should also be considered the provider of last resort to ensure that potentially excluded sections of the population are included. Decentralizing activities according to the needs of the communities or areas within the country is an important factor in generating new partnerships between employers and the various other sectors of the economy. This foregoing vision can be effectively reflected by the priorities that governments and their social partners accord the implementation plans and the resources allocated to education and training.

The responsibility for the initial basic and vocational preparation shall still remain primarily with the state, and can be designed to ensure employability and retrainability. It is important to expand and reform employment-based training to ensure articulation with institution based training through a national framework that includes individual learning credits banks and records, and the flexibility of multiple entry and exit points. In many countries the provision of TVE is the responsibility of several government ministries, and sometimes of different departments even within the same ministry. When the responsibility for TVE is shared in this way co-ordination mechanisms are required to ensure that the programme is truly national and efficiently conducted with appropriate linkages and articulation between and within different authorities and departments of the government. The role of employers, trades union and associations in TVE have been changing and growing. Large enterprises and professional associations are active in providing long and short TVE programmes.

The quality and effectiveness of such programmes may vary in the industrialized countries, countries in transition, and in those with stable or declining economic growth. The new vision for TVE should include facilitating the exchange of experiences, data and information on innovative approaches and new roles for employers, unions and professional associations. This could be achieved by creating information networks, and harnessing the multi-media information and communication technologies and data-banks. Employers could enhance their employee retraining programmes to upgrade skills by providing facilities for on-the-job training.

Voluntary organizations and non-governmental organizations (NGOs) make extremely valuable but often overlooked contributions to TVE. The role of NGOs in TVE has been changing dramatically during the last decade. Many NGOs have helped establish formal, non-formal, and informal education and training programmes. NGOs are also increasing their involvement in related areas such as poverty alleviation, employment generation, services for marginalized groups and empowerment of the disabled. TVE programmes are being used by NGOs as an important avenue for the afore-mentioned groups to acquire the knowledge and experiences demanded by the world of work.

TVE is thus perceived as an effective means of overcoming the social and economic difficulties encountered by these sections of society. The new roles that NGOs are now playing in the field of TVE must be acknowledged and enhanced in order that a new culture of lifelong learning is introduced outside the formal education system.

However, government and private sector must recognize that TVE is an investment, not a cost. It yields significant returns such as the well-being of workers, enhanced productivity and international competitiveness. Government, industry and other stakeholders must recognize both the monetary and non-monetary benefits of TVE. Funding for TVE must be shared to the maximum extent possible between government, industry, the community and the learner.

The human and financial resources allocated for TVE are sometimes diverted, in certain cases, to other parts of the system, which in turn affect TVE quality, effectiveness and efficiency to meet emerging needs. Governments must therefore streamline their institutional framework to achieve a coordinated national TVE system which involves partnership of both private and public partners. The role of donor agencies and funding institutions shall be enhanced and supported in the field of TVE, especially in the countries with social and economic difficulties.

The role of TVE institutions in finding partnership with business and industry in generating new project development require careful analysis. The benefits of these partnerships should be shared equitably by all the stakeholders. There are also opportunities for fund-raising and income-generating activities through collective effort. The mix will vary for each country. All partners in society will benefit from TVE and therefore they should assume the responsibility for the sustained vitality of their TVE system through cost-sharing mechanisms.

While the involvement of the private sector is growing in many countries, governments are responsible for developing and providing the necessary legislative framework. It is therefore essential for those of who have already embarked on this cause to proceed with even greater urgency and commitment. For those whose of who have not yet initiated this change it is necessary to start soonest and in earnest and to mobilise support and to explore the lessons of countries already on this road. There is a need for cooperation between developing and developed countries and countries with emerging market economies.

In Republic of Korea, technical and vocational education played a pivotal role in the rapid industrialization process. The government successfully restructured the vocational education and training system to meet the changing industrial demands. However, the country now faces new challenges posed by the changing global economic environment. In order to sustain its competitiveness, the Republic of Korea must now take active measures to reform its technical and vocational education programmes.

Technical and vocational education programmes within the formal education system are provided at both senior secondary schools and post-secondary institutions in Korea. Out-of-school vocational training is provided as non-formal education. Vocational senior secondary schools provide three-year programmes, preceded by six years of primary education and three years of junior secondary education. The programmes can be divided into six categories: agricultural, technical, commercial, marine and fisheries, vocational and comprehensive. The duration of field training varies, ranging from one to six months in agricultural and commercial schools, one to twelve months in technical schools and from three to twelve months in fishery and marine schools.

Vocational senior secondary schools are the major institutions for training the craftsmen and skilled manpower in the Republic of Korea. In 1997 there were 771 technical and vocational senior secondary schools with a total enrollment of 960,037, which accounted for about 40 per cent of the total senior secondary school enrolment. Junior vocational colleges provide two-year post-secondary programmes, with the exception of the marine and fisheries, and nursing courses which last two-and-a-half years and three years respectively.

In Korea, the purpose of junior college education is to produce middle-level technicians equipped with a solid base of theoretical knowledge and practical skills to meet the increasing demand for technical manpower following rapid industrialization. Specialized programmes are grouped into technical, agricultural, nursing, fisheries, health, commercial and business, home economics and so on. In 1997 there were 155 junior colleges with an enrolment of 724,741, about 28 percent of the total higher education enrolment. Non-formal vocational training comprises public and private training.

Public vocational training is undertaken by the Korea Manpower Agency (KOMA) under the Ministry of Labour and local governments. It aims to train semi-skilled and skilled workers through programmes lasting from three months to two years. KOMA manages institutes concerned with a broad range of occupations, while local governments concentrate on training in trades necessary for increasing the income of farm households. Private vocational training is conducted by enterprises and corporations.

Enterprises are required to pay employment insurance fees, the latter depending on the number of employees. The fees paid by the enterprises are pooled into a central fund, known as employment insurance funds, that are used to finance the vocational competency development programmes. The vocational competency development scheme, which came into effect in January 1999, replaced the compulsory training levy system. Private training is also carried out by corporations authorized by the Ministry of Labour.

The duration of vocational training programmes vary, ranging from short-term (hours, days, weeks) to long-term (six months to two years). The vocational training courses are divided into 'basic training', 'upgrade training', 'job transfer training', and 'retraining,' according to the objective of the training. The programmes are provided in 477 fields covering 23 technical areas.

During the year 1960s, the Republic of Korea was a typical labour-surplus economy with a modest endowment of natural resources and a small domestic market. The government established a vast economic development plan and restructured the vocational education and training system in order to supply the manpower necessary to implement the plan. As a result, most of the formal technical and vocational education was provided within the state education system, and was systematically planned and standardized. The government rapidly expanded enrolment in vocational schools in the 1960s.

However, the formal vocational schools were not able to prepare sufficient technical manpower for the rapidly industrializing country. In order to train enough workers to meet the increasing industrial demands, the government enacted the Vocational Training Law in 1967 as a result of which many new vocational training institutes were established. During the 1970s, the government undertook a fundamental structural change towards the development of heavy-chemical industries. This rapid structural change heightened the industrial demand for skilled workers and craftsmen. To meet this requirement, the government strengthened technical and vocational education at the secondary level, expanded the number of public vocational training institutes and legally mandated in-plant vocational training in most private enterprises.

The government encouraged private companies to provide in-plant training with the enactment of the Basic Law for Vocational Training in 1976. Large companies in certain industries were required to provide in-plant training for a certain number of their employees. These companies were obliged to pay a training levy if they did not provide in-plant training, or if their training did not meet government regulations. This mandate applied initially to firms with more than 500 employees; in 1991, this number was decreased to 150 employees, and in 1995 - to 100 employees in the manufacturing sector. In parallel with the rapid structural changes to heavy and chemical industries during the 1970s, the government re-organized the existing five-year junior technical colleges into two-year junior vocational colleges directed toward the preparation of technicians and engineers who are able to perform specific technical tasks in the heavy and chemical industrial fields.

In 1973, the government implemented the National Technical Qualification Testing (NTQT) system to improve the quality of skilled manpower and to enhance the socio-economic status of skilled technical workers. The system successfully encouraged students and employees to acquire higher technical and vocational skills, thereby effectively increasing the efficiency of the workforce. The Korea Manpower Agency and the Korea Chamber of Commerce and Industry (KCCI) were commissioned to carry out the National Qualification Testing. By the end of 1996, a total of 4,905,329 trainees had acquired national technical qualifications.

In the 1980s, the government expanded the opportunities for higher education to meet social demand, mainly for political reasons. The government strengthened the junior college education and established open universities to provide continuing education for the employed. Thus, enrolment in junior vocational colleges increased while enrolment in vocational senior secondary schools and the number of in-plant trainees began to decline. This resulted in a shortage of workers for production jobs, especially in the small and medium size companies. In the 1990s, the economy is facing new challenges posed by the changing economic environment including the globalization of trade and labour markets, the rapid advancement of new technologies and more competition.

Despite the expansion of higher education in the past decade, the present level of education and training is unable to meet today's industrial demands. The government has recently introduced various measures to strengthen the vocational education and training system in order to prepare the necessary skilled manpower to meet the changing industrial demands while reducing the pressure on higher education. In 1990, the government began implementing certain policies to increase the enrolment in vocational senior secondary schools, to increase the enrolment ratio of general versus vocational senior secondary schools from 68:32 to 50:50 by 1995.

In Korea, to strengthen the links between schools and industry, especially in the areas of technical education and training, a new system named "the Two-plus-one Program" was introduced in 1994 and was implemented in forty designated model schools in 1998. The programme comprises two years of vocational education in schools, followed by one year of practical 'hands-on' field training in industrial companies.

From 1999, the implementation of this system has been left to the discretion of technical senior secondary schools. Beginning in 1994, the Presidential Commission for Educational Reform (PCER) examined the effectiveness of the policies to expand enrolment figures for vocational senior secondary schools and to encourage close industry-school linkages. By the end of 1995, it was concluded that some of the earlier policy measures were inappropriate.

PCER recommended certain changes in the policies, placing emphasis on quantitative expansion of vocational senior secondary school enrolment to that of placing more emphasis on the quality improvement of vocational education. PCER proposed the Second Educational Reform Programme including the vocational education reform in 1996. Reflecting recent trends in higher education, the objective of the vocational education reform is to establish a 'Lifelong Vocational Education System'. In order to achieve this goal, legislation on the credit bank system in 1996 was enacted, allowing part-time registration to college on a test base system.

In short, students in vocational senior secondary schools and workers in industry are able to continue further education. These students have priority in the selection process for entry in colleges in related fields of study. With the introduction of a lifelong education system, the junior college education was expanded. Between 1979 and 1997, the enrolment in junior colleges increased 11 times and the programmes were diversified, from 91 into 361.

Based on the Educational Reform Programme, the customized training system responding to industrial demands has been implemented in two model junior colleges since 1996 and plans are underway to expand the programme. In order to strengthen the junior colleges' capacity for vocational education, programmes linking the curriculum of the second and third years of vocational senior secondary schools with that of the vocational college are being implemented in some pilot schools.

Students who have completed vocational senior secondary school courses are given priority in the selection process for entry into colleges in related fields of study. From 1996, the graduates of junior colleges receive associate degrees. As the required production skills became increasingly sophisticated with the manufacturing of higher value-added products in the late 1980s, companies began to emphasize skills upgrading for their workers while placing less emphasis on the initial training for trainees prior to employment.

Even though the compulsory training levy system contributed to the early increase of in-plant training, it failed to encourage companies to invest in the further education and training of their workers. To encourage enterprises to provide further training of those in employment, the government has introduced the vocational competency development scheme with the enactment of the Vocational Training Promotion Act in

1999. All companies with more than fifty employees are required to provide vocational competency development programmes for their employees and for job seekers. Since the latter part of 1997, the Republic of Korea has been suffering from ever-increasing unemployment.

The unemployment rate reached 8.0 percent in September 1998 as compared to 2.6 percent in 1997. Unemployment is expected to increase in 1999 due to the severe economic downturn, recent bankruptcies, and downsizing of many companies. Since the onset of the severe economic difficulties, the government has set up special training programmes for the unemployed as a social relief strategy. In July 1998, 3,079 training programmes were offered in 994 institutions.

The trends of globalization of trade and labour markets, rapidly changing technologies, and mass unemployment resulting from the recent economic crisis, are expected to continue in the twenty-first century. This trend will foster rapidly paced changes in future industrial structures and employment patterns. The effect on and changes in the labour market are that some jobs are declining in significance, others growing in importance and others still require completely new or different skills. The size of the workforce employed in the service and technology industries, where a high-level education and skills are required, will increase; while the demand for low-skilled workers will shrink.

Many employees are likely to change jobs, and possibly even careers, several times during their working lives. The changing nature of labour market trends has significant implications for education, implying inter alia the need to provide lifelong learning, continuing and recurrent technical and vocational education, and continued upgrading of knowledge and skills. In an effort to respond to the emerging challenges in the twenty-first century, the government will continue to implement current reforms. The following are measures and policy recommendations to be considered:

i) The common school curriculum should be revised to emphasize basic education rather than specialized education. Core competencies required for students should be identified and integrated into the Basic Common Curriculum from the first to the tenth grade, as proposed in the Seventh Curriculum which will be effective from the year 2000. Constant improvements in the area of knowledge and skills prove imperative for the future workforce to acquire the basis for developing further knowledge and skills as quickly and effectively as possible.

ii) Integration of the senior secondary school curriculum. Senior secondary schools willing to do so can integrate and manage the curricula of both vocational and general schools in order to enable students to choose from a wide selection of courses during the second and third year. This will enable students to satisfy requirements for further education while at the same time acquiring work-related knowledge and skills that will help them to enter the workforce. Schools that integrate and manage both curricula will minimize the number of compulsory courses which students must take and will increase the number of elective subjects.

iii) Lifelong education at different levels should be expanded to benefit each and every citizen. The educational trend has shifted so that more and more students are opting to.undertake further study beyond that of senior secondary school. Higher education institutes such as polytechnic universities, polytechnic colleges and junior colleges should therefore be strengthened and equipped as lifelong educational institutions allowing people of all ages to receive further occupational education. Flexible access to vocational education and training throughout life should be ensured.

iv) A School-to-work transition (STWT) system must be developed. STWT should begin in the earliest years of schooling, combining efforts in educational improvement, workforce development and economic development. The goal of STWT is to smooth the transition process for all students, including college-bound and non-college-bound youth, disadvantaged youth and out-of-school youth. The system seeks to find a balance in preparing students for "real jobs" without limiting their employment and school opportunities. The components of the system are:

   (a) work-based learning;

   (b) school-based learning;

   (c) connecting activities which articulate between the school-based and work-based components; and

   (d) career-awareness programmes.

v) Enterprise training should be encouraged. Companies, particularly those which invested in technology-intensive industries, require a continuous updating of skills and knowledge for which formal schools are inadequately prepared. Companies provide the best setting for workers to acquire the work-related knowledge and skills necessary to absorb future technology speedily.

International NGO Forum on Technical and Vocational Education

The International NGO Forum on Technical and Vocational Education was held on 27 April in the Congress Centre, organized jointly by KRIVET and UNESCO with the sponsorship of the Ministry of Education, Republic of Korea and UNDP.

The main theme of the Forum was "Strengthening NGO's role in developing technical and vocational education and international co-operation between NGOs". In his opening speech, Mr Power, Deputy Director-General for Education, UNESCO, said that "the outcome of the main Congress, of which this International NGO Forum is an important part, will certainly involve concrete follow-up and implementation plans in which partnerships with NGOs and the private sector will be of the essence, as the role of TVE itself is redefined and reshaped for the 21 st century".

The Forum discussed ways of strengthening their activities and examined the possibility of establishing an international co-operative network for the further development of technical and vocational education in each society. Five speakers and 4 designated discussants were invited to the Forum and included both representatives of NGOs and UNESCO.

The Forum was well attended, with approximately 120 participants, comprised of some 63 Korean national organizations, 45 representatives of around 20 international and regional NGOs, plus 6 UNESCO and other UN staff, and four representatives of UNESCO National Commissions and Member State delegations. At the close of the Forum, a set of recommendations was adopted which have been handed over to the Rapporteur-General of the Congress. The document containing these recommendations was included in those adopted at the close of the Congress. These recommendations reflect the concern of the above 120 Forum participants to ensure "new partnerships among NGOs, governments, professional association, trade unions and employer in order to improve technical and vocational education and training." The recommendations also urges UNESCO to "implement its new approach to co-operation with NGOs in order to strengthen and facilitate the functioning of NGOs working in accordance with the Organization's aims and field of competence".

Technical and Vocational Education and Training: A Vision for the Twenty-first Century (Recommendations to the Direct-General of UNESCO

Preamble

We, the participants in the Second International Congress on Technical and Vocational Education whose theme was Lifelong Learning and Training : A Bridge to the Future, meeting on the eve of a new century and millennium in Seoul, the capital of the Republic of Korea, a country which epitomizes the contribution of education to social and economic progress, have had the opportunity to work together in plenary sessions, commissions, round tables, and forums, to contribute to a world vision and programme for Technical and Vocational Education and Training (TVET) for the first decade of the new millennium.

We have considered the emerging challenges of the twenty-first century, a century that will be an era of knowledge, information and communication. Globalization and the revolution in information and communication technology have signalled the need for a new human-centred development paradigm. We have concluded that Technical and Vocational Education (TVE), as an integral component of lifelong learning, has a crucial role to play in this new era as an effective tool to realize the objectives of a culture of peace, environmentally sound sustainable development, social cohesion, and international citizenship.

Mindful of the opportunities that lie ahead of us and those which will progressively unfold, and cognizant of the policies, partnerships and resources needed to raise the status and broaden the traditional vision of Technical and Vocational Education, and recognizing the need for strengthened international partnerships particularly to address the needs of developing countries, we are forwarding the following recommendations to the Director-General of UNESCO and requesting him to submit them to the next session (30th) of the Organization's General Conference in view of its intention to launch a new global strategy for Technical and Vocational Education.

Theme I: The changing demands of the twenty- first century: Challenges to Technical and Vocational Education

1.1 The twenty-first century will bring a radically different economy and society with profound implications for technical and vocational education. TVE systems must adapt to these key features which include globalization, an ever-changing technological scenario, the revolution in information and communications, and the consequent rapid pace of social change. The implications of these transformations include the increased mobility of labour and capital, uneven impacts upon rich and poor, and emerging market economies in both rural and industrial sectors. The knowledge-based society which these changes are bringing offers exciting new modalities for education and training.

1.2 These social and economic trends predicate the need for a new development paradigm which holds a culture of peace and environmentally sound sustainable development as its central features. Accordingly the values, attitudes, policies and practices of TVE must have their foundations in this paradigm which will encompass inclusiveness and wider access, a shift to human development needs, and empowerment for effective participation in the world of work. Its focus must be on the needs and potential of the individual in society. TVE has a crucial role to play in this new paradigm by providing skills for all and should include the poor, the excluded and the unreached so that education remains an accessible basic human right. The universalization of TVE and the learning skill it imparts would enhance access to education for all citizens of the world. A new holistic approach is required so that education for the twenty-first century will include all domains of learning incorporating general and vocational education to enable the learner of the twenty-first century to launch into a lifelong continuum of knowledge, values and attitudes, and competencies and skills. The ultimate goal of such an approach would be the creation of a learning society.

1.3 Therefore TVE systems must be reformed to give life to this new paradigm by achieving flexibility, innovation and productivity, imparting the skills required, addressing the implications of changing labour markets, training and re-training the employed, unemployed and the marginalized with the objective of achieving equality of opportunity for all in both the formal and the informal sectors of the economy.

1.4 There must be a new partnership between education and the world of work to address the need to develop a synergy between the sectors of education and industry and the various other economic sectors, to foster the development of generic competencies, the work ethic, technological and entrepreneurial skills, and for imparting human values and standards for responsible citizenship.

1.5 There is a need to introduce the required changes in a manner suitable for each country, so as to empower and engage human beings in the context of the new paradigm, with TVE as a common key focus of the reform process.

1.6 The prerequisites of the TVE response to the new paradigm include appropriate societal values and attitudes, embracing the new technologies, making new policy and financial commitments, and taking account local, regional, and global opportunities and concerns. The sheer magnitude of the trends of the twenty-first century demands a political commitment and bold policy responses which are both regional and international.

Theme 2: Improving systems providing education and training throughout life

2.1 Lifelong learning is a journey with many pathways and TVE is an integral part of the voyage. Therefore TVE systems should be designed as developmental life experiences with cultural and environmental aspects in addition to their economic dimensions.

2.2 To make the maximum contribution to lifelong learning TVE systems need to be open, flexible and learner-oriented. They must do more than just provide the learner with knowledge and skills for specific jobs. They must also prepare individuals more generally for life and the world of work. TVE is for personal, social and economic benefit.

2.3 TVE needs to be based on a learning culture shared by individuals, industry, different economic sectors and government in which individuals are empowered to take progressively more responsibility for their own knowledge-management and independent learning while public and private providers ensure programmes that facilitate access to and through the pathways of lifelong learning.

2.4 TVE has an important role in reducing levels of anxiety in the midst of constant uncertainty by providing information and knowledge, skills and competencies, entrepreneurial capacity and the development of the human personality.

2.5 All nations require a coherent education policy and co-ordinated education systems within which TVE must be a fundamental part. TVE should develop close interfaces with all other education sectors, particularly schools and universities, to facilitate seamless pathways for learners. The emphasis must be on articulation, accreditation and recognition of prior learning to enhance their opportunities. Within this spectrum TVE has a responsibility to ensure a sound initial education and training aimed at learning to learn, the most precious skill for all citizens both young and adult.

2.6 Perhaps the biggest challenge which faces TVE is to co-ordinate the needs of a general and a vocational education through curriculum, pedagogy and delivery. Each country will wish to pursue its preferred approach to co-ordinate these domains but it is clear that the demands of the twenty-first century require new synergies between these fundamental pillars of education and training systems.

2.7 TVE should inspire in young people a positive attitude to innovation, enable them to help shape change and prepare them for self-reliance and citizenship.

2.8 TVE is particularly important in ensuring a seamless transition from the school to the workplace. To achieve this it needs an holistic approach which captures the dichotomies of the academic and the vocational, the theory and the applied, knowing and doing, the use of the head and the hand. This requires effective partnerships with schools and with industry and other economic sectors which embrace shared values, shared curriculum, shared resources, and shared outcomes.

2.9 The informal economic sector is often excluded in the spectrum of lifelong learning. TVE has a vital role to play in reaching out to this sector in every way possible to ensure that the less privileged have access to the pathways of continuous learning. This applies with equal force to those who drop out of the formal cycle of education.

2.10 To achieve all of these aspirations for Technical and Vocational Education a number of urgent considerations must be addressed:

— the status and prestige of TVE must be enhanced in the eyes of the community and the media. This includes raising the status of teachers in TVE systems through attention to their own skills and competencies and the provision of resources for their task. It will also require strong marketing of the capabilities of TVE to its many stakeholders, accompanied by a simplification of TVE in the minds of many who find its language, its products and its modalities too complex. Publicizing and disseminating models of good practice in TVE are also important. There is a need to promote parity of esteem between vocational and general education, especially in developing countries;

— the sectors of education must achieve more effective interrelationships to facilitate more seamless pathways for learners. They do not need to be homogenized; each sector can retain its identity and they all can recognize each other's passports and visas at their borders;

— there must be flexibility in programme administration and curriculum design to facilitate a smooth passage through lifelong learning and provide continuous entry, exit and re-entry points;

— career guidance and counselling is of the utmost importance for all clients of the education and training systems and needs to be significantly strengthened. Career guidance should take into account the needs of industry, the individual and the family and be sensitive to each learner's requirements and circumstances. Its role should be extended to prepare students and adults for the real possibility of frequent career change which could include periods of unemployment and employment in the informal sector. It should not only be a recognized function of educational institutions but should also be provided at other venues accessible to the population at large;

— all stakeholders, particularly industry and educationalists, must be involved in new TVE partnerships. Each has much to learn from the other in approaches to lifelong learning;

— the high cost of many TVE programmes must be addressed. They should be redesigned to incorporate more workplace learning;

— the lifelong learning continuum will be best sustained if there is a diversity of funding, a diversity of providers, and a diversity of delivery mechanisms. Innovative approaches to flexible delivery of TVE including the use of information and communication technology and distance learning should be particularly welcomed;

— quality assurance is essential to ensure a new higher status for TVE. Qualification standards, certification processes, valid assessment methods and acceptable outcomes are all key ingredients and should be the hallmarks of all TVE systems;

— We need to understand more about the critical moments of choice on the journey of lifelong learning. More research should be encouraged to help understand the key issues, dilemmas, potential barriers and opportunities which confront the voyager at the various phases of the journey. More longitudinal studies would be of significant benefit in this regard.

Theme 3: Innovating the education and training process

3.1 The challenges facing the learner of the twenty-first century demand innovative approaches in TVE. This is seen most clearly in the need for a re-oriented curriculum to take account of new subjects and issues of importance. Obvious examples would include technology, the environment, the understanding of foreign languages and cultures, entrepreneurial capacity and the requirements of the rapidly growing service industries connected with leisure, tourism and hospitality.

3.2 The rapid pace of change also introduces the prospect of a virtual curriculum whereby learners must be prepared to cope with the obsolescence of their knowledge and skills, and the introduction of new elements which have yet to appear in common usage. They must also be prepared for a radically new labour market in which traditional wage-employment may be the experience of only a minority and self-employment in various forms may offer a high potential for economic independence in a new era of entrepreneurship.

3.3 The new information technology has opened up a whole new potential in technology-based learning. It should be possible to use and apply simple as well as modern technology and the new information and communication technologies in the TVE teaching and learning process without losing the valuable aspects of traditional teaching methods particularly the personal nature of the teacher-learner relationship. Technology-based learning should play a crucial role in the development of a culture of lifelong learning with the capacity to empower learners by providing them with multiple new pathways to meet their education and training needs.

3.4 The new technologies must be harnessed to provide widespread access to TVE. They should be used to make distance irrelevant and to render curriculum-based knowledge and vocational guidance information more easily accessible to all. They have the potential to offer flexibility in time and location to TVE delivery, and should enable TVE to function as a catalyst for the penetration of new technologies in underdeveloped regions of the world, particularly in rural areas.

3.5 As the workplace calls for more sophisticated skills, a sound basic education must be provided as a prerequisite foundation for TVE. This should involve the acquisition of more complex competencies in school, including enhanced literary and numeracy skills and the ability to understand and communicate through the tools of modern technology.

3.6 Since technology comes at a price, ways must be found through partnerships with industry, financial and aid agencies, regional and international co-operation, to address the high costs involved, especially for developing countries. New ways must also be found to share intellectual property for the benefit of learners in all countries and situations.

3.7 Given the essential need for innovation in TVE, the role of the teacher remains paramount. New methods must be found for the initial training of teachers accompanied by the continuous upgrading of their competencies and professional development. A rethinking must take place as to the qualifications required of the TVE teacher of the twenty-first century, including the optimum balance of training acquired on the campus and in the work place. They must be assisted to develop new and appropriate instruments of assessment, accreditation, articulation and certification standards.

3.8 TVE needs an early global warning system and more futuristic studies to enable preparation for changes in the work place and in society. Industry must be involved with Governments and research centres in identifying the knowledge, skills and competencies which will be required by the changing economy so that TVE systems can adapt. The prospect of competencies applicable across regions and internationally should be addressed to respond to the projected escalation in resource mobility in the next century.

Theme 4: Technical and Vocational Education for all

4.1 TVE is one of the most powerful instruments for enabling all members of the community to face new challenges and to find their roles as productive members of society. It is an effective tool for achieving social cohesion, integration and self esteem.

4.2 TVE programmes should be designed as comprehensive and inclusive systems to accommodate the needs of all learners; they must be accessible to all. Special efforts are needed to reach previously marginalized groups. Where specialized programmes are required, these should be designed to facilitate entry into the mainstream, thus ensuring continued access to lifelong learning.

4.3 The list of recognized marginalized groups is becoming longer and there are certain to be others which are yet unknown. TVE programmes, both formal and non-formal, must be made available in varying modes of accessible delivery, to the unemployed, early school leavers, out of school youth, those disadvantaged by distance and location, rural populations, indigenous people, those in the midst of urban despair, populations engaged in informal labour markets with poor working and living circumstances, children working under hazardous conditions, refugees, migrants, and demobilized soldiers in post-conflict situations.

4.4 The under-representation of women in TVE is of particular concern. Traditional perceptions of appropriate roles for men and women in the work place should be challenged. TVE must respond with gender-inclusive learning programmes, both in content and delivery, including measures to attract men into previously female-dominated training and careers. Faculty need to be gender-sensitive.

4.5 For the promotion of equal access of girls and women to TVE courses, more effective forms of educational and vocational guidance and counselling must be provided, along with gender-sensitive guidance and counselling materials. At the same time the learning and working environments must be made more suitable for the participation of girls and women, overt and covert bias and discrimination must be removed, and a positive image and appropriate incentives for female participation in TVE should be created.

4.6 To overcome the lack of employment opportunities for girls and women, and the misconception that they are incapable of performing particular tasks, TVE programmes emphasizing the development of their entrepreneurial capacity should be undertaken.

4.7 The journey through lifelong learning is burdensome for the disabled; the pathways are very rocky and difficult to negotiate. Their aspirations and achievements must be broadened. People with disabilities frequently have difficulty accessing TVE for a range of reasons. These include the underestimation of educators and vocational guidance personnel of the ability and potential of people with disabilities to take up competitive paid employment. Those who are able to join mainstream TVE programmes should be assisted to do so while those with more severe disabilities should be provided with special programmes and learning strategies to realize their potential and optimize their participation in society and the work force.

4.8 The commitment to TVE for all requires well designed policies and strategies, increased resources, flexible and appropriate delivery modes, friendly training environments and sensitive and caring teachers and employers.

Theme 5: Changing roles of Government and other stakeholders in TVE

5.1 Although governments carry the primary responsibility for TVE, in a modern market economy TVE policy design and delivery must be achieved through a new partnership between government, employers, vocations, industry, trades union and society. This partnership must create a coherent legislative framework to enable the launching of a national strategy for change. Within this strategy the government, apart from actually providing TVE, can fulfil the roles of giving leadership and vision, facilitating, co-ordinating, establishing quality assurance and ensuring that TVE is for all through identifying and addressing community service obligations. The capacities of the partnerships must be enhanced through training schemes and facilities to impart appropriate skills.

5.2 The new partnership should aim to establish a learning culture throughout the society whilst strengthening the economy, achieving social cohesion, helping to maintain cultural identity and diversity and the enhancement of humanity. Training for all occupations directly related to human development should include human rights and responsibilities. The learning culture should enable the establishment and maintenance of an institutional structure which will achieve lifelong learning, wider participation in education and training, and foster the work ethic with a revitalized spirit of entrepreneurship.

5.3 Both the monetary and non-monetary benefits of TVE should be recognized by government, industry and other stakeholders.

5.4 The contribution of the voluntary and NGO sectors to the provision of TVE must be recognized and supported because it constitutes an extremely valuable but often overlooked resource.

5.5 Government and the private sector must recognize that TVE is an investment, not a cost, with significant returns including the well-being of workers, enhanced productivity and international competitiveness. Therefore funding for TVE must be shared to the maximum extent possible between government, industry, the community and the learner. There are also opportunities for fund-raising and income-generating activities through collective effort. The mix will vary for each country, but it is important to realize that the benefits of TVE are for all of the partners in society who should therefore take the responsibility to contribute to the creation and ongoing vitality of their TVE system through cost sharing, incorporating appropriate government financial incentives.

5.6 A vibrant economy is best served by a diversity of public and private providers of TVE operating in healthy competition, within a national framework of quality assurance. The balance can be struck in many ways but the government should assume responsibility for ensuring strong basic initial vocational preparation no matter which sector is providing its delivery. Government should also be considered a provider of last resort to ensure that potentially excluded populations are not overlooked and are ensured access to TVE programmes. There is a particular need in all countries to expand employment-based training which is well articulated with institutional training through a national framework which includes individual learning credit banks and records, and multiple and flexible entry and exit points. The private sector has a particularly important role to play in this regard.

5.7 Within governments there are often shared and overlapping responsibilities for various elements of TVE amongst departments and agencies. It is desirable that governments streamline their own public institutional framework to the maximum extent possible to co-ordinate the national TVE effort, create an effective partnership with the private sector and promote TVE for the benefit of all stakeholders.

5.8 All TVE partners will be required to increase constantly their knowledge and expertise in many areas affecting TVE systems. Effective mechanisms must therefore be established to share experience and expertise through ongoing research of particular relevance for key policy issues. Other approaches may include jointly shared data banks, multimedia technologies, and regional and international co-operation.

5.9 There is significant scope for countries to share their experience with the design and operation of national TVE policies and strategies, and appropriate public and private roles and partnerships. In this regard there is a need for mutual and co-operative assistance between developing and developed countries and those countries with emerging market economies.

Theme 6: Enhancing international co-operation in TVE

6.1 There is an urgent need for more financial and technical support from international agencies for education, and Technical and Vocational Education in particular, to allow TVE to contribute more significantly to economic and social development.

6.2 Further co-operation is encouraged between UNESCO and its international partners such as the ILO, The World Bank and the Regional Development Banks, OECD, the European Union and CEDEFOP, the European Training Foundation, ISESCO, the Commonwealth, La Francophonie etc. to enhance TVE, with UNESCO assuming a co-ordinating role through its comparative advantage in the various fields of education.

6.3 There should be increased co-operation between the North and the South, as well as between countries of the South, to renovate and sustain TVE systems, including through research and development.

6.4 The needs of developing countries require specific recognition, particularly in areas such as investment in TVE, the provision of basic education including literacy and numeracy skills to facilitate access to TVE, the encouragement of ownership of TVE and the increase of their budget for TVE.

6.5 International financial authorities must recognize the contribution of education, and particularly TVE, to the maintenance of peace and stability and in preventing social dysfunction, and should incorporate the support of TVE in their conditions for assistance to recipient countries.

6.6 UNESCO's efforts to develop a strategy for TVE for the first decade of the twenty-first century are strongly supported. The UNEVOC network should be strengthened. Member States are encouraged to continue to underpin regional and national Centres which are essential vehicles for the achievement of the new vision for TVE in the twenty-first century. The Congress strongly recommends that UNESCO increases significantly the budgetary allocation for its TVE programme activities to ensure the successful implementation of the new strategy. To encourage such a revitalization of TVE in the new century, UNESCO should also consider the establishment of an international prize for innovation in TVE.

6.7 In the light of the new expanded vision for TVE, which has been endorsed at this Congress and which stresses the need for incorporating a new relationship between the various sectors of education and training, an holistic approach to the preparation for life and the world of work and increasingly seamless pathways in lifelong learning, the Congress recommends that the Director-General of UNESCO, in close collaboration with the ILO, develops a common concept of Technical and Vocational Education and Training (TVET), to guide the UNESCO strategy for the twenty-first century.

5

Distance Learning: Promises for the Future

Distance education is a system of rational actions for the imparting of knowledge, skills and attitudes, whereby the originally direct social relationships between teacher and students are substituted to a great extent by indirect relations which are characterized by technical rules and prescriptions, a context-free language, conditioned prognoses and conditioned instructions, goal attainment with the help of target-means relations, and the systematical increase of effectivity.

Distance education produces neither funny teaching characters nor notoriously annoying types of students, as is often the case in face-to-face instruction. The systems of distance education are, it is true, 'standardized in order to raise their functionality', and 'production in series', 'mechanization', and 'functionalization' and 'functionalization' are their important structural traits. Finally, it should be mentioned that the motivation of many distant students derives from a 'materialistic attitude towards life' - that,is, that they strive to improve their conditions of life by obtaining higher qualifications. While this attitude may be a general one in our time, it seems, however, to be typical in a special sense for distant students.

When we consider new arguments - for instance, those of Jochen Kaltschmid, who has proved again in a profound analysis that 'the apparatus, the technicalization, mechanization, division of labour and organization' are all elements of the process of rationalization which shape the existence of man, and that the consequences of this rationalization are that our world is 'dominated by purposes', that we lose our 'inwardness', the 'immediacy of life' and the unity of our psychological faculties - then, of course, we have to see that these consequences, indeed, are very likely to be reinforced by industrialized education. In fact, its rationalized systems of teaching and learning are, as we have seen, structured in such a way that the purposes - the defined teaching goals - are achieved in the best way, the 'inwardness' of the students and the teachers, which is normally preserved by their personal interaction, is more or less lost by the objectivation of teaching behaviour, the splitting up of teaching and learning functions, and by the use of technical media. Also, the 'closeness to life' of instruction is, naturally, reduced a great deal.

Teachers and students are no longer involved as whole human beings. And the unity of our psychic faculties is broken up. There are also many current argument about the incompatibility of technical developments and education which are often emotive and relate to the concept of instrialized education, as this form of education is - as we have shown - a result of the general process technicalizing of society. Ludwig Heieck has discussed some of these arguments. According to him, education gives way to the functionalist thinking in terms of expediency in our technical age and abandons man. He says: 'Education derives from history. It is determined by the view that man is a historic being. Technical progress, however, is a historic. Instruction and education, therefore, have not participated in technical progress as they have felt threatened by it'. And he concludes : 'If man abandons himself to the world of materialistic objects, if he delivers his humanity to the functionality of set purposes-then he dehumanizes himself'.

If this treatise shows that distance education has developed so to speak unnoticeably—as industrialized education during the last 120 years, and if, over and above, it is maintained that this model of education will be of great importance for tackling important educational tasks at present and in the future, then it is necessary to comment on the reservations voiced by those critics of culture as they would otherwise underline that such a concept will be questionable, if not dangerous.

We have to face the same situation which was characterized by Paul Heimann, when he defended his contention that 'film, radio, and television are the powerful educational institutions of the present'. The objections raised to their educational use in the past also apply top distance education, especially when it employs such mass media.

According to Heimann, these critics were afraid of 'the furtherance of a receptive learning behaviour, an educational and instructional impressionism, the emergence of a dangerous conformism, the immobilization of creative imagination, the artificial increase of optical and acoustical stimuli, the reduction of primary experiences in favour of secondary experiences, the depersonalization, the mechanization of the relation between teacher and taught, and the leveling out of individual instruction'. Heimann emphasized that these objections must by no means be trivialized, as some of them contain important arguments of educational philosophy. On the other hand, his reflections led to the conclusion that these objections can scarcely be refuted on the level of pure educational thinking. Therefore, he offered arguments dealing with problems of intellectual history and sociology.

Distance education provides necessary technical and organizational preconditions for a universal admission to continued and higher education. An analysis of statistics about distance education reveals that millions of distant students do indeed profit from this industrialized way of education. Often enough it offers them the only way towards the desired education as all other ways are barred by lack of funds or by other circumstances. Comparison with the conditions under which face-to-face-instruction takes place in the schools of the Federal Republic of Germany as well as in those of other countries can be used to show that we are dealing with school systems organized according to class structures in which access to secondary schools and universities remains restricted, so that people continue to suffer from the inequality of educational opportunities.

Distance education is mainly dependent on indirect interaction and communication it has, so to speak, completed its seculization. The interaction between teacher and student is objectified by rational teaching techniques and the use of technical media to such a degree that even relicts of archaic attitudes are no longer possible. In instructional face-to-face situations, however, one can still find them. The traditional teaching and learning behaviours are obviously so stable that they resist the use of technical media and the application of principles of industrialization. The communicative structure of traditional instruction in the classroom depends on limited number of students. Probably 120 students would be the largest possible number in a lecture hall. A radical new approach was needed to overcome this limitation and to make possible the instruction of large and extremely large groups of students which appeared when the general level of education had to be raised as a consequence of industrialization. Distance education is such an approach. The archaic forms of imparting knowledge and skills could be characterized with regard to their media structure by the negative statement that they functioned without any technical medium. This means that the teachers relied on the medium of the words spoken directly to the student. Whether the teacher was a medicine man, a prophet, a shaman or a priest, he or she always communicated knowledge orally. The oral teaching of those priest-teachers must, however, not be understood in a modern sense, as the words were not yet isolated from their original context.

Today, distance education developed considerably further by becoming largely independent from the traditional ties. This opens up new perspectives which have not yet been noticed and new problems which have not yet been tackled by experts of the methodology of teaching and learning. The six lines of development show clearly that distance education is a form of instruction which reached the final stages in each dimension only because it applied principles of industrialization.

1. Distance education can be egalitarian, as the application of technical media overcomes some of the traditional barriers to educational opportunity. These media enable schools and universities to extend their

instructional systems in such a way that every capable citizen can profit from learning if they wish - even after their school or college years. In the present historical -economic situation of highly industrialized societies the increased availability and accessibility of education thus assumes a special importance, as the further democratizing of society will increase the educational needs of all citizens considerably. More and more of them will lay claim to their human right of education. It is safe to say that such an increased demand of education can only be satisfied with the help of industrialized forms of education.

2. Distance education provides for instruction in which teaching and learning have been secularized to a high degree, as the relation between teacher and students has been isolated from its traditional social context and objectified. Teacher and students do not interact as persons in their totality, but as special teaching and learning functions which operate only in order to reach the defined goals. The numinous, however, needs the social context in order to be able to express itself.

3. Distance education enables and facilitates instruction without repressive actions in the sense that arbitrary acts of teachers - as well as of students - are cut out as technical mediation and the required division of labour have objectified instruction. If there are institutional or direct dependencies, as, for instance, in the military services and in vocational training, they will be less effective for the same reasons.

4. Distance education is a form of instruction which is capable of catering for great numbers of students and even mass audiences. Such a form of instruction

would be impossible without the techniques of industrial mass production and without the help of mass media and the computer.

5. Distance education is principally mediated instruction. It cannot take place without the help of technical media. Without the mechanization of the presentation of the contents of instruction and of the feedback activities it would not be possible to start, optimize and control it.

6. Distance education has cut the three bonds which ties face-to-face instruction to special places, special times and special persons. The industrial approach of objectifying teaching and learning behaviour and of storing, transporting and reproducing it was the required precondition for this. It has made distance education the most accessible and flexible form of teaching and learning. On the whole, and with regard to the objections of the cultural critics referred to at the beginning, the interpretation of the historic model of instruction results in the conclusion that the tradition of instruction has not been disturbed or even neutralized by the advent of industrialized education. On the contrary, it subsequently developed along the lines of development in the history of instruction.

Distance education can be assigned to the era of industrialization not only because of the availability of the necessary material and technical conditions, but also because of particular socio-cultural and intellectual developments which are imperative before distance education can emerge. If in our society many adults and adolescents decide to study at a distance and not in the traditional way, if they manage to go their own way and do not depend on the traditional educational institutions, they must have qualities which distinguish them from people who lived in earlier eras., It is elucidating to analyse these qualities. A first precondition is a particular relationship between humans and their environment. Human consciousness of the environment has changed in along process which stated with archaic-mythological ways of thinking which were gradually replaced by empirical-realistic ideas and concepts. This process was accentuated by the Renaissance and the Enlightenment as they helped to emancipate human thinking from earlier limitations. At this point it is sufficient to indicate which of these developments were important in the context of the hypothesis presented at the beginning. In the Renaissance, many people became aware for the first time that education can be also used for secular purposes. There was a growing need for the establishment of town schools and of an urban education. In the era of the Enlightenment, teaching and learning were secularized even further. People were inspired by the image of the individual who is able to change unsatisfactory conditions of society by means of reason.

Distance education is normally characterised by affective neutrality—as here the teaching and learning is not achieved by an interaction of persons, but, strictly speaking, of isolated functions. As Fairs also suggested, this does not necessarily mean that technically mediated instruction cannot be affective at all. Now and then one can find initial stages of it. Generally speaking, however, it remains safe to say that in distance education the social relations tend to be neutral. Traditional instruction in the classroom is oriented to a particular frame of reference: a given teacher teaches a given learning group in a given temporal and locational situation. Industrialised instruction, on the other hand, disregards particular conditions of this kind, as it has a more general, if not principally universal frame of reference. Distance education tends, indeed, towards universal application.

Distance education , uses a language which is taken out of its originally associated surroundings, and is thus free of its context. The technically mediated communication of necessity remains unaffected by particular circumstance, as it addresses students everywhere. In the classroom the communicative acting is determined by reciprocal expectations of behaviour. This means that the teacher who acts expects the students to react in a special way and vice versa. The expected reactions take place with a higher degree of probability the more the interacting persons have internalized a role consensus and the more the expected behaviour has become ritualized by habit.

In industrialised distance education the segments of interaction are constructed on the basis of conditioned prognoses and conditioned imperatives. Again, particular sequences of a global behaviour become objectified and isolated. In face-to-face instruction the dominant mechanism of acquisition is the internalisation of roles. The students live up to expectations by internalising the norms of the group. Knowledge and skills are transported by means of this particular role identification, role taking and role performance. In distance education, however, the teaching-learning process is reduced to the learning of skills and qualifications. Every measure in this system has the sole function of achieving this goal. Communicative action and role performance are cut out. In face-to-face instruction the social interaction helps to maintain the institution. Teachers and students are subject to external and internal control. In distance education, however, the indirect interaction is subject to the attainment of the learning goals by using means to an end. Correspondingly, the reactions to breaches of the rules are different in the two subsystems.

Distance Learning Programmes

Distance learning has become an option because of the increasing availability of higher-speed, two-way digital telecommunication facilities. Fibre based terrestrial networks are available in most US markets and advances in digital video compression means that a "low-end" DS1 line is adequate for many distance learning applications. In addition, satellite-based networks cover nearly the entire US although two-way connectivity is difficult to achieve directly, a return path can be secured using a dialup voice/data line. The bottom line is that the growing availability of connectivity options is positively influencing educational institutions' adoption of distance learning. The road to the goals of an equitable, technology-rich education system requires a number of initiatives.

Interactive Distance learning (IDL) is one the technological tools that can contribute to the solution of the educational problems that society faces. IDL refers to a portfolio of application and networking solutions that can be (and are being) implemented by universities, K-12 schools, corporations, and government agencies to enable them to enhance the education and research process. IDL solutions establish telecommunication links between education receivers and various sources of knowledge over geographic areas that may span a metropolitan segment, a whole state, or the entire country. These sources of knowledge are not limited to distance learning providers, such as universities and corporate training centres; they also encompass information and processing resources, such as libraries, supercomputer centres, and museums. The required links may involve voice communications, video communications, data communications, or a combination of these media. The quality of the distance learning programmes is a function of the selected type of solution and the particular needs of the distance learners.IDL solutions can address many of the challenges facing education and training institutions. Educators and administrators who appreciate the positive value of telecommunications are investing school capital and operating funds in IDL technology; in many schools and colleges, telecommunications has become a line item in the operating budget.

New technologies, namely satellite communication, fibre optic cable and computers have dramatically enhanced educational capabilities. By providing communication links, telecommunications can overcome distance barriers that hamper development. Thus through the use of new communication technologies, access to good educational programmes can be greatly extended to large audiences in rural and remote areas with tremendous flexibility in subject matter content and in locations served. Corollary to these technological expansions, the area of education which is considered to be fastest growing today is that of distance education. Distance education, based on the use of modern communications and multimedia materials, has proved to be the major new movement in human resource development in the current decade. The ability to cope with rapid changes in the higher education system will become the primary measure of success, of both micro and macro levels, as we approach the 21st century.

Many societies have shifted from industrial era to information era, and others are fast moving in that direction. The volume of information that becomes available, doubles every four to five years. Teachers have to become experts in helping learners navigate through this sea of information rather than pretending to be effective transformers of that information into knowledge. Students must be trained to bring about that information. Those who survive this information explosion will be able to deal with it effectively and even more importantly, acquire knowledge. Education is going to be number one amongst the great world industries, within which will flourish an educational machine technology that will provide tools such as the individually selected and articulated two-way TV and an inter-continentally networked documentary call up system operative on any home two-way set.

Emergence of the information technology including the satellite-based telecommunication system has generated a potential of a sea-change in the education system all over the world. Print, radio, television, audio-video cassettes, tape-recorders, overhead/slide projectors, filmstrips, etc., which permit only one-way communication have become old educational technologies and have lost novelty in the developed world. The last one decade has seen emergence of a series of new, electronic-based innovations in the field of higher education, which permit vision, sound, data with inter-activity. Information highways are high speed data networks used to transport information and link people who want to be connected with others. Teletext and Video-text are the two new information age services that will soon be widespread among home and business users. Teletext is a one-way service in which pages of information from a central database are broadcast on a regular television signal. Video-text is a more sophisticated two-way service using telephone lines. E-mail, tele-conferencing (audio and video) and computer conferencing are common activities on the internet and other electronic networks. The words information highway reflect speed, volume, powers, and efficiency. With the information highways becoming a reality in many countries, Conferencing Technologies (CT) have come to be used in a large way in collaborative distance and open learning. The success of CTs will depend on the extent to which learning tasks, such as attentiveness, idea generation, concept elaboration, feedback, etc., are fulfilled. The CTs reduce the teachers' teaching functions without reducing the academic rigour. Since generally the adults are the participants of CTs, a collaborative type of learning is necessary. When integrated into the whole learning context, CTs offer sufficient flexibility to the learners and the educators. Thus, a virtual classroom can be created in which the class is taught using the satellite, microwave or cable linkages between them.

The electronically linking of students and teachers at various locations by cable, microwave or satellite has made it possible to create this face-to-face teaching at a distance. There is no doubt that an extensive emergence of electronic-based technology in the field of education is in the offing. However, one must not forget limitations in its use, especially in the developing countries. The advocates of the modern technologies in education presuppose that the learners have access to a wide range of high specification information and communication technologies; that these technologies can be used at time and in circumstances that are convenient for learners and optimal for effective study; and the learners have sufficient familiarity or experience of using them. Unfortunately all these presumptions are far from true so far as learners in developing countries are concerned. Though there may be television in the house, there is certainly a claim of all members of the family for using TV for entertainment purposes. Not many students have access to VCRs because of the costs. Even those who have VCRs may not always be able to use them in view of the competing demand for TV time by others. PC and modems are absent in most of the learner houses in the developing countries.

Multiplicity of languages used in the same country, as in India, also poses severe problems in reaching distance education to different parts through the broadcasting/networking systems. Thus, there are severe limitations in the use of high specification informa-tion and communication technology in the developing countries. It may take two to three decades to reduce these limitations to an insignificant level.It will be difficult to protect national, state or provincial boundaries from distance education. Governments will have to deal with the question, sooner or later, whether they would like to be net exporters or net importers of education. The answer of course is quality.

The distance teaching institutions, in particular, will have to demonstrate superior quality of education that will override the public's preconceptions of the status of better- known, more conventional institutions as they enter into the distance teaching world via the internet. There is also the question of access. The high specification information and communication technology can be accessed only by the rich and the very rich in the developing countries who can afford to have a number of TVs, modems, computers and can afford to pay for long distance call charges, etc. separately for entertainment and education purposes. The proportion of such learners is microscopically small. Since they belong to the elitist society they would, anyway, have been well educated in the conventional system of education.

Electronic-based technologies will dominate the education scenario in the developed countries. The 21st century will give rise to electronic educational institutions which will provide information on education and training needs and opportunities; quality control; accreditation; coherent curricula and other concomitant services. Many of the instructors or tutors may not belong to the educational institutions but will be independent contractors. Nor would it be necessary for learners to be registered with an educational institution.

The educational institutions may only collect and deliver payments for fees and royalties to the owners of the software or the telecom companies. Unless the less developed countries are able to create an appropriate technological infrastructure to support the kind of learning needed in the 21st century, they would be left far behind. Building up of information highways are the *sine quo non* of the modern system. The need of the 21st century will be to exploit the information highway to the fullest possible extent.

In order to make education accessible to all and to make it meaningful, exciting and interesting, a new technology need to be linked with the process of learning. The new technology is not only capable of overcoming the barriers that distance presents, but also changes the very nature of the instructional process. It is technology that made the move from correspondence to distance education possible. If the demands of the society for education are to be met successfully, we will have to switch over to an alternative approach of unconventional mode of distance education through mass communication technology currently available.

Modern communication technologies have the potential to bypass several stages and sequences in the process of development encountered in earlier decades. In order to avoid structural dualism, modern education technology must reach out to the most distant areas and to the most deprived sections of beneficiaries simultaneously with the areas of comparative affluence and ready availability. Media is a kind of message of delivery system which includes all kinds of mechanical devices directed to educational use. These devices are used as means of communicating our ideas to large number of people who are located in far off areas.

Choice of media is crucial where there is no provision for face-to-face interaction and the students depend on print material with occasional face-to-face support. Distance education programmes can be enriched and made more attractive, effective and satisfying by using a variety of media relevant to the content for learning and the facilities that can be provided should attempt an exploitation of the potential of the variety of powerful media provided by modern technology. The educational media was confined to classroom lectures supported by print material.

Education was imparted with the help of maps, charts, pictures, books, diagrams and till recently through using 11 mm projectors for educational purposes. Actually the 1970's were the decade of print. The present day mechanical devices have brought about a virtual revolution in diverse field of human activity. A variety of media are used in distance education in open universities as well as in institutes of distance learning. They can be classified into two groups:

(a) print media and

(b) non-print media.

Print media: Distance education cannot do without printed course material. It is the mainstay of the instructional system almost everywhere. It is in the form of reading material or in the form of programmed instructional material. It is the most popular medium because it is easy to carry, is comparatively cheaper and can be used according to the convenience of the learners. The learners get the self- instructional material at their homes by post. The material is carefully prepared by experts in the field of their expertise to suit the needs of the learners and to help them learn the subject without much assistance from others.

Non-print media: The area of non-print media includes the technologies such as radio and television, telephone, videotex, computers, internet, satellites and so on.

Radio: The radio has become one of the most powerful media of mass communication in the modern age. It is being increasingly used in advanced countries to overcome the shortage of qualified teachers and suitable books. It can enrich the farthest corners. If the radio has become a necessary instrument of education in advanced and progressive countries, the services it can render are still far greater in a country like India. As a matter of fact, the radio is an effective medium and has been extensively used for educational purposes to spread literacy or to give formal or non-formal education all over the world. In addition to the printed materials lessons are planned and written for broadcast from All India Radio. Radio programmes supplement and reinforce instruction imparted through the printed material. The radio is within the reach of the common man and can be carried along from place to place.

Television: The television is a more effective medium than radio for spreading education, because the language of TV is rich, powerful and expressive. TV lessons are entertaining as well as attractive. A lesson received through the gates of eyes and ears has a double chance of retention by learners.

Audio-video cassettes: The audio/video cassettes can be played and replayed at home by the learner at his/her will. A learner can stop a particular tape at a point where more details are necessary and can play in slow motion to understand a difficult point. He need not get up early in the morning or wake up late in the night for radio and TV broadcasts. The use of video enabled a good lecturer to be seen and heard all over the country, without having to repeat his performance. At the moment, the video equipment is costly in India and even in other developing countries and they are not within the reach of most of the students.

Telephone: The telephone is a very effective means of communication. It offers two ways interactive communications across distance, i.e., people can talk to each other, discuss and ask questions. In India this is unlikely to be considered as a medium in distance education.

Videotex: The videotex makes home television sets to function like a computer terminal and retrieve text information and graphics from a remote database. It gives much wider access to information and much wider ease with which new concepts and ideas can be transmitted.

Computers: The mass teaching system has become virtually impossible without a computer. The computer is a very good tool to improve the process of teaching and learning. It is of tremendous use for teaching and learning in diverse situations. Computer based instructions include a broad range of applications. The major classification of computer application for distance learning are "Computer Assisted Instruction and Computer Management Instruction". The target number of students must be large because of the special skills and time required to develop effective computer-aided instruction.

Internet: The internet is the largest, most powerful computer network in the world. It encompasses 1.3 million computers with internet addresses that are used up by 30 million people in more than fifty countries. As more colleges, universities, schools, companies and private citizens are connected to the internet either through affiliations with regional not-for-profit network or by subscribing to information services provided for profit companies, more possibilities are open for distance educators to overcome time and distance to reach students. The easy availability of computers and worldwide internet has brought about significant changes in learning-teaching strategies. The present electronic communication system has made the interaction much easier and essentially less costly. With the access to internet, distance educators and their students can use the Electronic Mail (E-Mail), Bulletin Boards and World Wide Web (WWW). The WWW and web browsers have made the internet a more user-friendly environment.

Satellite: The satellite is the glamourous medium in distance education. It is used for communicating over long distance. More channels for both radio and television are possible because of the satellite. Programmes are viewed by people in cities as well as in countryside locations. The satellite and television network offers a powerful medium for the dissemination of knowledge, cultural programme and developmental information. A wide area is covered without any loss of quality in the messages sent. The communication channels are not affected by natural calamities as is usually the case with telephone wires. All teaching and learning programmes can be greatly improved by visual and auditory materials because these make the learning experience far more concrete and memorable. But the media has remained under-exploited by the distance learning system for want of appropriate and relevant software which is the greatest problem of this system. India is making a mark in distance education and we need to develop and grow a large number of efficient, committed and trained media persons to implement new technologies in this field.

While distance education is already a fact of life for most universities and an increasing number of community colleges, knowing the intrinsic problems and overcoming them will be critical to successful implementation of distance programs on a larger scale in the future. In distance learning students and teachers will find themselves playing different roles than is the norm in traditional education. The teacher is no longer the sole source of knowledge but instead becomes a facilitator to support student learning, while the student actively participates in what and how knowledge is imparted. More than any other teaching method, distance learning requires a collaborative effort between student and teacher, unbounded by the traditional limits of time, space, and single-instructor effort. Advances in telecommunications technology has opened up the possibility of personal and group interaction in distance education. Both computer and audio conferencing permit the introduction of class discussions without the group meeting face to face. Phone calls and electronic mail replaces personal office visits.

The distance learner can now have almost the same instructional contact and interaction as the student on campus. But remote access education does not need to eliminate all the benefits of human contact. In fact, the proliferation of the modem, teleconferencing, and the World Wide Web provide a rich expanse of both information and contacts that were previously unavailable. Albeit two dimensional, these media lend themselves to pure ideas and thought processes.

The improved access and availability of electronic technology has enabled more adult students to participate in the learning process. Students who enroll in distance learning courses do so for convenience. They are either time-bound due to work or travel schedules or location-bound due to geographic or family responsibilities. Distance learning is student-centered learning; thus knowing the characteristics and demographics of the distance learners helps us understand the potential barriers to leaning. Problems and barriers encountered by the student fall into several distinct categories;

— costs and motivators,

— feedback and teacher contact,

— student support and services,

— alienation and isolation,

— lack of experience, and training.

Costs and motivators: More so than traditional students, distance learners are more likely to have insecurities about learning. These insecurities are founded in personal and school related issues such as financial costs of study, disruption of family life, perceived irrelevance of their studies and lack of support from employers. These pressures often result in higher dropout rates than among traditional students.

Feedback and teacher contact: Because there is not daily or weekly face to face contact with teachers, students may have trouble in self-evaluation. Keegan believes that the separation of student and teacher imposed by distance removes a vital "link" of communication between these two parties. The link must be restored through overt institutional efforts so that the teaching-learning transaction may be "reintegrated". Citing Tinto, Keegan hypothesized that students who did not receive adequate reintegration measures such as electronic or telephone communication, would be less likely to experience complete academic and social integration into institutional life. Consequently, such students would be more likely to drop out. These barriers can be mitigated through technological methods such as e-mail. Computer conferencing and electronic mail can be integrated into the delivery of the course to provide the missing interactivity. Because both are essentially asynchronous, they continue to leave the student in charge of setting his or her own work times—a critical success factor for the distance student. It is important that the student receive prompt feedback in any institutional setting, particularly in distance learning where the learner is impaired by the lack of casual contact with the teacher and other students. This is especially important for those students who live outside metropolitan areas. They may not have access to reliable telecommunications, computers, and postal mail. The frustrations resulting from problems with communication between student and academic institution are factors of which distance education planners should be well aware.

Student support and services: The isolation that results from the distance learning process can complicate the learning process for adult students. Support for distance learners should not be overlooked when planning distance programs. Students need tutors and academic planners to help them complete courses on time and to act as a support system when stress becomes a problem. Planners from Washington State University (WSU) note that "student services are a significant part of the budgeted costs of the program." They also believe that " success in attracting, serving, and retaining students will hinge more on excellent student support services than on any technology issues.". Technology costs and considerations can be a source of budgeting problems; however, student support for distance learners should take precedence.

Alienation and isolation: A fourth problem area is the feelings of alienation and isolation reported by distance students. Students of all kinds want to be part of a larger school community, and simply a member of a "correspondence" course. For many traditional students, this is an important part of their social lives. The "distance" aspect of distance learning takes away much of the social interactions that would be present in traditional learning environments. This problem must be mitigated by institutions providing a sense of personal involvement between the student and the institution. One way to help solve this problem is through the use of tutors that communicate with students either electronically or by phone. Students believe that having a good tutor is vitally important in helping them get the most out of a course and achieve a credit. Geographical isolation has been identified as one of the major problems for distance students. In addition to the practical problems of contacting academic and administrative staff, obtaining study materials and borrowing library books, distance students suffer from the disadvantage of being unable to interact with other students and are often denied the perception that they belong to a scholarly community.

Lack of experience, and training: If distance learning institutions are serious about providing equity of educational opportunity to all, then careful consideration must be given to the special needs of students undertaking distance education for the first time. Of particular importance is the design of study materials for distance students. Study materials must take into account the significant proportion of students who enroll with little or no experience of distance study. These students are at risk of dropping out unless they develop study survival skills as rapidly as possible.Another problem encountered by students is the lack of student training, particularly in reference to technical issues. Many adult students are not well versed in the uses of technology such as computers and the Internet. Using electronic medium in distance learning can inadvertently exclude students who lack computer or writing skills. These skills are required if computer technology is used. Students will typically be offered volumes of electronic-based information. Using this information will be a problem for some non-technical students.

6

Education: Designing and Building Future Programmes

India is one of the few countries where, during the stabilisation phase of structural adjustment, expenditure on education has been stepped up. Achievements during the last 56 years are not insignificant. An estimated 95 per cent of the rural population living in 8,26,000 habitations have a primary school within one km and about 85 per cent population have an upper primary school within three km. More than 150 million children are currently enrolled covering around 90 per cent of the children in the age group of 6-14 years. Recent surveys on literacy rates indicate a pheno-menal progress in the nineties.

Basic education policies and programmes in the recent years have gone beyond the mere emphasis on numbers to focus on quality concerns in basic education, on the education of girls and disadvantaged sections of the society, the need for people's involvement in basic education programmes and decentralisation of educational management. It is also during this period that World Bank and other international donor agencies began providing additional funds for speeding up the process of universalisation of elementary education.

Despite such significant achievements and positive goal orientation in the recent years, it is realised that there are serious problems of gender, regional, sectional and caste disparities in UEE. A significant proportion of students continue to dropout due to socioeconomic and cultural factors as also due to lack of adequate infrastructure, shortage of teachers and unsatisfactory quality of education provided. The country still is the home for more than 300 million illiterates.

Though the progress made is not insignificant, the country realises that the challenges ahead at the turn of the century are quite daunting, demanding not only continued commitment but also an enhanced attention and resources to meet the challenges in the coming years. The government is fully seized of the fact that nothing less than a wholehearted national effort both in the public and private sectors would be necessary if India is to emerge as a fully literate and economically vibrant nation of the 21st century. The task before the country is to orchestrate the demand among the marginalised and underprivileged sections of the society through effective micro-level actions. The 1990s witnessed many successful attempts in this regard. Several EFA projects such as *Lok Jumbish* as well as the literacy campaigns have also demonstrated tremendous potential of collaborative efforts between government and non-govern-mental organisations. On the whole, one can say that recent years have witnessed closer involvement of the civil society in EFA activities and have consequently increased public awareness and political attention towards EFA.

However, three lines of action taken by the government during the last decade are indicative of a positive political ambience in the country worth mentioning. The first set of actions relate to certain major legislative measures initiated in the recent years. One of them is the formulation of a bill for making education a fundamental right of every citizen. The bill which is under examination if adopted by the parliament will make the government legally res-ponsible for ensuring education of all children up to the age of 14 years as already specified in the Indian Constitution as a directive principle. Some states are also going for additional legislative measures. For instance, Tamil Nadu has passed a compulsory education act with all necessary clauses for enforcing universal participation of all children in primary education. Another legislative measure adopted in recent years relates to the constitutional amendment on panchayati raj institutions following which some states have initiated radical measures for decentralising primary education man-agement. Another aspect which also indicates a positive orientation of the political leadership towards EFA is that of increased allocation for EFA. In reality, the resources available for basic education may not be adequate. However, the efforts made in the last few years to provide increased allocations for primary education in comparison to other sectors of education is a significant point to note.

Despite all the problems and challenges that the system faces, recent EFA project initiatives in the country have clearly demonstrated the capacity of the country to move forward towards the goal of EFA, both in terms of continued commitment at the policy level and availability of human resources necessary for implementing various policies and programmes in the field. It is an impossible task to make any meaningful assessment of the overall progress made in India towards EFA goals during the post-Jomtien period. One can at the most characterise the progress as a mix of considerable success coupled with yet unsolved riddles. Improvement in the provision of basic education facilities in the country has been a gradual process and sufficient space had already been covered even before the 1990s. A major step forward taken during the recent years is to make primary education practically available at the doorsteps of the children. This is being done by creating institutional facilities in smaller habitations with the help of the local community moving away from the traditional norms of distance and population size. This step could prove to be major step forward in bringing marginalised sections of the population into the fold of basic education.With improved provision, enrolment and participation of children has also grown.

One of the most positive trends observed is regarding the decreasing disparity between male-female enrolment figures as well as literacy rates. The traditional resistance to education of girls seems to have been at least partially overcome possibly due to major advocacy carried out through literacy campaigns and through over-actions to improve women's status as a whole. However, the process seems to have just begun and there is still a long way to go. A related factor, which appears to be not fully tackled, is the persistence of low participation of certain marginalised groups and geographical pockets. It is not that efforts have not been made in this direction. But the issue, perhaps, calls for closer scrutiny and redesigning of the strategies adopted in the past. Quality improvement has, no doubt, come to occupy the centre-stage of all EFA efforts during the last decade. Large investments have been made to upgrade the infrastructure and human resource position in the primary schools across the country. Though external funding has contributed significantly in this direction, it is important to note that a large part of the overall investment has been from domestic resources. Apart from increasing investment, several concrete steps have also been taken to improve the quality of learning and teaching in primary schools.

Massive efforts for training of in-service teachers has been initiated during the last ten years. This coupled with the specification of 'minimum levels of learning' at the national level has, in general, heightened the awareness of all concerned people towards improving learner achievement levels. India began its journey towards the goal of Universal Elementary Education (UEE) for all by opening more and more primary schools across the country. Today nearly four out of five children in the age group 6-14 years are in school. Two out of three persons are functionally literate. Progress achieved is by no means small. But it falls short of meeting the goal of Education For All (EFA). In the pursuit of the goal of providing basic education for all, the National Policy on Education and the follow-up actions on the recommendations of the policy in 1986 has been a major landmark. The World Declaration on Education For All adopted soon after in 1990 gave further boost to the various processes already set in motion in the country. As the analysis presented in the document demonstrates, the last decade of the century has witnessed tremendous progress in the area of basic education in the country. Yet, it is realised that the journey is not yet over. The main task is not to lose the momentum created by the progress made in the last decade. It is necessary to consolidate the gains and capitalise on the enlarged base created by the progress. It is realised that the methods hereto adopted may not be appropriate for crossing the difficult hurdles in the last leg of the journey towards EFA. The strategy has to be such that the goal is achieved within the first few years of the next century. To achieve the goal of universal elementary education in the years to come have to measure up to the magnitude and complexity of the task which has so far remained incomplete. Recognising the importance of the primary education sector, the central government has been working with the state governments on a principle of shared responsibility for achieving the goals of UEE. This becomes even more important in the context of the commitment to make 'right to elementary education' a fundamental one.

Broad-based efforts made during the last 50 years have resulted in a massive expansion of the education system in the country, raising the overall status of educational provisions in terms of accessibility and participation. The efforts were guided by concerns of equity. Yet, a closer analysis of basic statistics reveal glaring disparities in the progress made.

Developments in Basic Education

The national policy envisages Early Childhood Care and Education (ECCE) as a holistic input fostering health, psychological and nutritional development of children. The Integrated Child Development Service (ICDS) is the largest programme under ECCE. It is an inter-sectorial programme which seeks to directly reach out to children from vulnerable and remote areas and give them a head start by providing an integrated programme of health, nutrition and early childhood education. Its package of services includes supplementary nutrition, immunisation, health check-up, referral services, non-formal pre-school education and community participation for children below six years and to pregnant and nursing mothers. The scheme is funded by the central government. Though ICDS is the major programme catering to the ECCE needs, several other schemes have also been initiated by the central and state governments mainly to supplement the ICDS provisions, in content and coverage. For instance, 'Creches and Day Care Centres Scheme' was started in 1975 to provide day care services for children below five years. Similarly, 'Early Childhood Education Scheme' was introduced as a distinct strategy to reduce the dropout rate and to improve the rate of retention of children in primary schools. Under this scheme, central assistance is given to voluntary organisations for running pre-school education centres. In addition to these schemes that reach out to the rural, urban slums and tribal areas, there are innumerable private, fee charging nursery schools which cater to the needs of the parents living in urban and semi-urban areas.

At present, there is no system of licensing or recognition of such institutions. During the last 10 years, the ICDS has been expanded considerably. For instance, during 1992-95, 911 new blocks were brought under the scheme bringing the total coverage of blocks under the scheme to 3,072. The ICDS scheme has been universalised during 1995-96 through sanction of projects for all the 5,320 community development blocks, and 310 major urban slums thus increasing the total number of sanctioned *Anganwadis* to about 7,98,000. The spread of ECCE facilities, particularly in terms of ICDS centres, has been phenomenal during the recent years co-vering all the 5,320 community development blocks in the country.

However, the actual outreach and coverage in respect of early childhood education component has been rather poor. Further, the coverage is very uneven across different parts of the country. Proper understanding of the variations in the levels of participation of children in the ECCE facilities will require additional data related to different dimensions of community life and development, viz., demographic, social, cultural, political and economic. Apart from the quantitative expansion of facilities, there have also been efforts to create alternative models of ECCE under different EFA programmes. The efforts made in this direction particularly in the States of Assam, Madhya Pradesh, Rajasthan, Andhra Pradesh and Karnataka are worth mentioning.

There have also been attempts to create convergence between the ongoing programmes of ICDS and the early childhood education activities, essentially by expanding the scope of the ICDS programmes. The challenge in extending the ECCE facilities to all children is enormous and has to be made an integral part of all EFA projects in the years to come. Another point emphasised in this regard is to strengthen the linkage between early childhood education programmes and primary education programmes. Towards this end, many state governments are establishing pre-primary units attached to primary schools. Inter-sectorial convergence and co-ordination is crucial for the success of any ECCE/ECE programme and its linkage with primary education. Setting up of state level coordination committees by state governments to prepare state specific plans is being promoted as a viable convergence strategy. Considering the difficult socio-economic conditions in which a large number of people particularly in rural areas live, it has been the endeavour of the government to provide primary schooling facilities within easy access of all children. Though this may imply providing smaller schools with relatively less facilities, it is considered that expecting parents to send their children long distance for centralised schooling facilities may prove counter-productive.

The number of primary schools increased nearly three times between 1951 and 1991. The increasing trend has continued, perhaps with greater vigour, during the last decade. This has, no doubt, helped spread basic education in some of the remote corners of the country. However, this may not indicate whether the entire population and habitations in India have been adequately covered/served by basic schooling facilities within reasonable distance as prescribed for the children of these age groups. As seen from the data presented, facilities for primary schooling had been made available within their neighbourhood for 93.76 per cent population of rural habitations, by 1993. Only about six per cent population in rural habitations did not have such facilities within the norm of one km distance. The accessibility to the facility of primary schooling has further increased after 1993, as more than 27,000 new primary schools were established during the period from 1992-93 to 1996-97. There is another relevant fact about the population of these rural habitations without access to primary schooling. While 45.25 per cent of these are having a population less than 300, about 40,000 habitations have a population of 300 or more which have to be provided by primary schools as per the norms referred to earlier in this section. Thus, provision of primary schools to unserved small habitations became a major concern during the 1990's and considerable success could be achieved in this regard in some of the states.

The Education Guarantee Scheme (EGS) initiated by the Madhya Pradesh government has demonstrated how a demand-based provision with the comm-unity at the centre-stage can help in much faster progress. Under the scheme, any community, which has a group of at least 25 school-going age children, can demand from the government to provide a primary school within their habit-ation. As a reciprocal measure, the community has to find a place for conducting the school and also ensure the attendance of the children enrolled in the EGS school, as consistently low attendance would lead to closure of the school. Similar efforts based on micro-planning and school mapping exercises have been attempted under *Lok Jumbish,* the EFA project in Rajasthan.

Other major projects such as DPEP have also focused on improving the access to primary school facilities in remote and unserved habitations. Schooling facility at the upper primary stage has also increased over the years. The facilities of upper primary schooling, though widespread, are comparatively less accessible, as the norms for establishment specify a radius of three kms. Eighty-five per cent rural population has facilities for upper primary schooling within a distance of three kms. In terms of rural habitations, upper primary schooling facilities are available within the habitation for 76.15 per cent.

The access to upper primary schooling has improved considerably as 23,000 upper primary schools (middle schools) were established during the period from 1992-93 to 1996-97, indicating an increase of 14.8 per cent, raising the per cent of rural population served by upper primary section to 90.95. Mere existence of schooling facility does not guarantee the participation of children in schooling.

This is clearly brought out by the large variations among the states/UTs in respect of access to elementary education. For instance, the highest percentage of unserved population by a primary school/section within one km distance, is that for Himachal Pradesh, though this is a state with literacy rate much above the national average. In contrast, in respect of Bihar, the percentage of population unserved by primary school/section is only 4.49 which is quite low comparatively, though Bihar has the lowest literacy rate in the country, viz., 35.1 which indirectly indicates that a large section of the population has not been making use of the schooling facility available.

Enrolment in primary level of education has increased by about six times between 1951 and 1997 while the enrolment in upper primary level increased by about 11 times during the same period. The increase in case of girls had been nine times in primary level, and 24 times in upper primary level. The annual compound growth rate of enrolment in primary classes has been 3.76 per cent while in case of upper primary level, it has been 4.06 per cent per annum. The primary school system in India has grown in size consistently reaching an enrolment of nearly 150 million. This poses a major challenge not only for efficient management but also for mobilising resources needed to maintain even a reasonable level of quality.

Though the enrolment of girls has grown at a much faster rate than for boys during the last ten years, the difference continues to be very large with only six girls for every eight boys in the school. Though the size of total enrolment in schools is very impressive, the population growth during the last few decades has also been high. The most important indicator pointing to the participation of children in schooling is the enrolment ratio. Gross enrolment ratios have remained relatively static during the decade. Corresponding figures for girls show an increase of about six percentage points. One of these is the fact that children are not enroled exactly at the official age specified by the State, which also varies from one state to another.

Special enrolment drives carried out to bring even older children into the primary schools have also influenced the age composition of the school-going population. Seventeen states/UTs have a lower NER than the country's average while fifteen states/UTs have a higher NER than the national average. Whatever be the reasons for slow growth and even if computation methods are responsible for certain amount of under reporting, the enrolment ratios indicate the major challenge that the country faces in bringing all children to school. In the 1990s the Gross Enrolment Ratio (GERs) both for boys and girls at primary stage are getting stabilised. Comparability of Net Enrolment Ratio NER with net attend-ance ratios also indicates to the stability being achieved in terms of enrolment and attendance pattern. The central and state governments have initiated several special measures for the problems of regional and gender disparities. Mere provision of access and enrolment of children in the school are not enough for achieving the goal of education for all. These should be coupled with suitable measures to ensure that children stay in the school to complete the full cycle of primary education. Though most states of India have done well in enrolling more and more children in the school, lack of capacity of the schools to retain the children in the school has been a serious problem. Regular information on dropout and retention of children is not collected in all the states. Therefore, getting an accurate data on the regular participation level of children in the schools and their progress through various classes to completion of the full cycle is not possible to compute as this is also affected by failure rates.

Several special measures have been implemented to bring all children to school and retain them for the full cycle of primary education. The goal of EFA is to bring all such children into the fold of primary education. In 1997, 35.06 million children of the age group 6-11 years were out of school. Therefore, the net additional enrolment of this order will be required in order to achieve the goal of EFA. The data clearly show how varied the requirement is among different states. One can also observe that the bulk of the children to be enroled are in a few educationally backward States. Of the additional net enrolment of 39.25 million, a large portion consisting of 30.45 million children are estimated to be in eight states, viz., Andhra Pradesh, Bihar, Gujarat, Maharashtra, Madhya Pradesh, Orissa, Uttar Pradesh and West Bengal. There are large segments of children from marginalised groups continue to be deprived of primary education. Recognising the need for providing alternate means of reaching primary education to such children a programme of non-formal education (NFE) was launched by the government nearly two decades ago. The NFE programme caters to the learning needs of children in the age group, 6-14 years who remain outside the formal system of education for a variety of reasons. These include dropouts of the formal schools, children from habitations without schools, children who assist in performing domestic chores like fetching fuel, fodder, water, attending to siblings, grazing cattle, etc., and girls who are unable to attend formal schools. The programme has been revised and strengthened during the 1990s. Though the original scheme was meant only for ten educationally backward states, it has been extended to cover urban slums, hilly, tribal and desert areas and projects for working children in other states also.

The programme is characterised by flexible features that facilitate spread of basic education among traditionally disadvantaged sections of population. It has consistently grown in size and coverage for two decades. In particular, a significant expansion of the programme took place during the 1990s in terms of the number of NFE centres and the number of children enroled in them. By 1997, there were 2,79,000 NFE centres covering about seven million children in 21 states. Of these, 2,40,747 are being run by state governments and 37,808 by 544 NGOs/ voluntary agencies. Five states, viz., Uttar Pradesh, Bihar, Andhra Pradesh, Madhya Pradesh and Orissa account for 81 per cent of the NFE centres. The spread of NFE programme is moderate in Rajasthan and Assam. Coverage is very limited in Jammu and Kashmir, and North-eastern states; the programme started in Arunachal Pradesh during the 1990s. The government of India has been giving liberal grants to support such activities by NGOs. Participation of voluntary agencies in NFE has increased phenomenally during the 1990s.

While there were 7,310 NFE centres run by voluntary agencies in 1993, their number swelled to 37,808 in 1996 and to 58,788 in 1999. Besides running NFE centres, these NGOs have been implementing 41 experimental and innovative programmes for promoting elementary education. The NFE scheme has given rise to a number of innovative experiments by NGOs as well as other implementing agencies. Almost all the major EFA projects have evolved different approaches and institutional arrangements for reaching primary education to the disadvantaged within the broad framework of NFE. Some of these are the 'Sahaj Siksha programme' under *Lok Jumbish* in Rajasthan and the Alternate School Programme under DPEP in Madhya Pradesh.This aspect of the scope provided by NFE for promoting pluralism and variety in design and delivery of primary education needs further attention from policy makers and planners.

During the 1990s, two features of the NFE programme were stressed. These were importance of making necessary investments in qualitative improvement of NFE, and reiteration that the advantages of NFE lay in its flexibility and adaptability to the needs of disadvantaged children. Evaluation of the NFE programme has also made several useful suggestions for streamlining the organisation of the NFE scheme, improving infrastructure, qualitative improve-ment in various inputs and their monitoring with a view to increasing the internal efficiency of the NFE system and enhancing its effectiveness. NFE is a low-cost alternative to formal primary school. However, findings of evaluation of the scheme do not lend support to this assumption. The revised programme of NFE has to aim at delivering literacy, numeracy and awareness to those out-of-school children who cannot be brought to the formal education system and not cost saving. This approach places a greater challenge on the government for raising adequate resources for the NFE programme.

Redefenition of Universalisation of Elementary Education (UEE) in the National Policy on Education—1986 consisting not only of enrolment and attendance but also of learner achievement brought focus on quality of primary education in a significant manner. The emphasis laid on achievement indicators by the Jomtien

Declaration gave further impetus to this and brought quality concerns and improvement in learner achievement to the centre stage of policy making and planning for basic education in India.There is no single factor solution for the problem. Quality improvement in education cannot be carried out on a turnkey basis in a prespecified timeframe. Persisting with efforts to move ahead on all fronts mentioned in the strategy above is seen as the most important factor. Keeping this in view a number of programmes and schemes have been initiated by the central as well as state governments.In the traditional framework for providing classrooms and teachers, number of students has been the main determining factor. Under this framework, small schools located in remote areas and invariably serving marginalised groups suffer from serious inadequacies. Breaking away from this framework, following the recommendations of the NPE, a national programme called 'Operation Blackboard' was launched around 1990 to equip every school with certain basic infrastructure and human resources. The government of India has spent on an average about Rs. 400 million per year during the last ten years on this scheme. More than 1,82,000 classrooms have been built and 1,49,000 additional teachers appointed.

Besides, 42,000 posts of tea-chers have been sanctioned to add a third teacher to primary schools with more than 100 enrolment. A standard set of school equipment has also been supplied to all primary schools. This is in addition to the teacher augmentation and construction of school building done by state governments through various state level schemes further, the EFA projects have also given considerable importance to improvement in infrastructure including repair and maintenance of school buildings. An important dimension of this whole exercise is the element of community involvement.

In most cases, under DPEP as well as *Lok Jumbish,* emphasis is laid on the role played by community members through village education committees or special school building construction committees. For instance, more than 5,000 new school buildings are to be constructed in the seven DPEP states. With the expansion of educational facilities, the number of teachers has also increased over the years. The policy of the government is to provide two teachers to every primary school initially and ultimately the endeavour is to provide one teacher for every class or section in primary schools. In the upper primary schools the teachers are provided on the basis of subject teaching and teaching workload. The specification of Minimum Levels of Learning (MLL) in early 1990s at the national level also prompted the states to take up the task of curriculum and textbook revision. A series of activities in all the states with EFA projects as well as others were set in motion.

In spite of additional teachers being appointed in many project schools, the majority of the schools in the country—around 80 to 85 per cent, adopt multi-grade teaching. This, perhaps, is inevitable with more schools in smaller habitations being opened. Adapting to such conditions and making the teaching-learning process still effective is a big challenge faced by a primary school teacher. This has been the main focus of all the EFA initiatives in the country. A major project initiative called *Shikshak Samakhya* (Teacher Empowerment) was initiated in the early 1990s in Madhya Pradesh with UNICEF support, which emphasised teacher creativity and autonomy for classroom organisation and teaching with a view to making learning a joyful experience for the children. The experiment has influenced the pedagogic renewal process in many other states, viz., *Ananddayi Shikshan* in Maharashtra and *Guru Mitra Yojana* in Rajasthan. Similarly, following the model evolved by the Rishi Valley Education Trust in Andhra Pradesh, a small effort was made for resetting the teaching learning process in a block in Mysore district. After extensive trailing and adaptation to local conditions, the DPEP in Karnataka is attempting to extend the initiative to other districts in the state.

The National Policy on Education (NPE) recommended decentralising the technical and academic support mechanism by establishing a District Institute of Education and Training (DIET) in each district exclusively to cater to the development needs of elementary education of the particular district. The establishment of a DIET in each district following the NPE-1986 was a major step in taking the support system nearer to the field. During the last ten years more than 400 such district level institutions have been established. This process of decentralisation has been further extended under the externally aided EFA projects through the establishment of Block Resource Centres (BRCs) and Cluster Resource Centres (CRCs). The main function of these sub-district level institutions is capacity building among teachers.

Partnership between government bodies and NGOs with field experience in teacher training is another important feature of the in-service teacher training programmes in the recent years. For instance, *Lok Jumbish* has been working very closely with *Sandhan, Allaripu and Digantar* and several other NGOs in their programmes for teacher capacity building as well as for training of other field level personnel working for quality improvement in school functioning. The *Rajiv Gandhi Shiksha Mission* which implements DPEP in Madhya Pradesh has been taking the help of *Ekalavya.*

Developments in Adult Education

The neglect of education during colonial times combined with social distortions had made the quest for learning a rather difficult and daunting task especially for those belonging to underprivileged social groups.

The rationale for the establishment of the National Literacy Mission (NLM) lay in the realisation that the process of nation-building would never be complete without giving literacy a major thrust. It was on this account that the NLM was launched in the mission mode with a clear time frame to achieve the objective of making 100 million literate in 15-35 age group by 1999. The success of the Ernakulam model (a district in the State of Kerala), which based itself on a spirit of voluntarism and complete mobilisation of civil society, became the organising principle of the total literacy campaigns.The district is the unit of implementation and coverage of all the blocks in a district taken up in campaign mode with people's participation. Over the last five years, the campaign has been expanded to remote corners of the country including the educationally backward states of Bihar, Madhya Pradesh, Uttar Pradesh and Rajasthan. The spirit of voluntarism has been remarkable in the literacy campaigns. Even, inaccessible districts such as Dumka in Bihar and Banswara in Rajasthan, with very low female literacy levels in 1991, have generated significant social mobili-sation campaigns and have unleashed unprecedented enthusiasm across the country. The NLM meets the challenge of monitoring by periodically providing for external visits to campaign districts and by generating performance reports in a simplified format.

Concurrent evaluations are under-taken when at least 50 per cent of the enroled learners who have completed the first primer. Final evaluation of TLC campaigns are undertaken when at least 60 per cent of the enroled learners have either completed the third Primer or are nearing completion. Authentic information on literacy rates at the national level are available only from the decennial census held in the country. Inclusion of literacy as an important variable in the recently held national level sample survey by the National Sample Survey Organisation has made it possible to get a picture of the progress made between 1991 and 1997, as also a comparison of the progress made in the previous decades. It is important to look at progress in literacy in a long-term perspective as changes in adult literacy figures are not dependent only on literacy activities but also on the efficiency and effectiveness of school education programmes.

The growth of literacy has been quite steady since 1951. It shows a remarkable jump after 1991. While the average decadal growth rate has been only 10.3 per cent, between the period 1991 to 1997 has registered an increase of about 10 per cent. Extrapolation of this growth rate, indicates that the country with little more intensive effort could cross the critical point of 70 per cent by the turn of the century, five per cent short of the threshold target level set by the NLM. This, no doubt, is a remarkable progress made in a relative short period of time.

The total population of the country has been raising at a fast rate and as the estimates indicate, it has already crossed the billion mark.Though the literacy rate had also been consistently increasing it could not keep pace with the population growth rate.

Consequently, the number of illiterates went rising for several decades. In fact, the reduction in the number of illiterates between 1991 and 1997 has been quite substantial indicating the success of efforts made in the decade in the area of literacy and basic education. One can see that this gap which was very wide is getting gradually reduced.

The rapidity of growth of literacy in rural areas, as opposed to urban areas, is markedly more in the last six years as opposed to any previous decade. This is possibly due to quicker progress in primary education that picked up in the earlier decades as well as due to the unprecedented participatory mobilisation process initiated through the total literacy campaigns in the 1990s. The single biggest characteristic of the literacy campaigns has been their ability to galvanise entire communities into believing that learning must become an integral part of their lives.

The *modus operandi* has been to create and build an environment conclusive to learning by accessing communities through their cultural roots and traditions. Enrolment of boys and girls in the age group 5-15 years is significantly higher in neo-literate households as compared to children in illiterate households.

Two out of three boys in neo-literate households are enroled in schools compared to three out of four in participant households. The biggest achievement of the adult education movement has been its impact on girls' education. The confidence of the girls as they perform their scholastic and extracurricular roles is the result of the awareness among neo-literate parents that girls need to be educated and outgoing.

The need to provide equal opportunity to both girls and boys has also had the effect of generating greater demand for the quantity and quality of primary schooling.The great strength of the adult education programme has been the involvement of women. As much as 62 per cent of participants in India are female. Programmes have provided illiterate adult women who have been denied access to formal schooling with great opportunity for reading, writing, increasing awareness levels and skills training.

Literacy and adult education campaigns have actively promoted gender equity and have sought to empower them as to decision making about themselves, their families and their communities.This major strain running through the programmes has played a significant role in improving the status of women within their own families. Whereas, traditionally women in India had little say in family decision making, they, through participation, have begun to express their newly found self-belief in having a say both within and without the family.

Adult education has helped spread knowledge about health care and nutrition, thereby enabling mothers to keep their families in better health and to care better for their children. India has initiated a series of new programmes and projects during the last 10 years to meet the goal of EFA. Each project or programme has set specific targets and also incorporated various monitoring and evaluation mechanisms.

National Policy on Education, 1986

PART I

INTRODUCTORY

1.1 Education has continued to evolve, diversify and extend its reach and coverage since the dawn of human history. Every country develops its system of education to express and promote its unique sociocultural identity and also to meet the challenges of the times. There are moments in history when a new direction has to be given to an age-old process. That moment is today.

1.2 The country has reached a stage in its economic and technical development when a major effort must be made to derive the maximum benefit from the assets already created and to ensure that the fruits of change reach all sections. Education is the highway to that goal.

1.3 With this aim ill view, the Government of India announced in January 1985 that a new Education Policy would be formulated for the country. A comprehensive appraisal of the existing educational scene was made, followed by a countrywide debate. The views and suggestions received from different, quarters were carefully studied.

The 1968 Education Policy and After

1.4 The National Policy of 1968 marked a significant step in the history of' education In post-independence India. It aimed to promote national progress, a sense, a sense of common citizenship and culture, and to strengthen national integration. It laid stress on the need for a radical reconstruction of the education system, to improve its quality at all stages, and gave much greater attention to science and technology, the cultivation of moral values and a closer relation between education and the life of the people.

1.5 Since the adoption of the 1968 policy, there has been considerable expansion in educational facilities all over the country at all levels. More than 90 per cent of the country's rural habitations now have schooling facilities within a radius of one kilometer. There has been sizable augmentation of facilities at other stages also.

1.6 Perhaps the most notable development has been the acceptance of a common structure of education throughout the country and the introduction on the 10 + 2 + 3 system by most States. In the school curricula, in addition to laying down a common scheme of studies for boys and girls, science and mathematics were incorporated as compulsory subjects and work experience assigned a place of importance.

1.7 A beginning was also made in restructuring of courses at the undergraduate level. Centres of Advanced Studies were set up for post-graduate education and research. And we have been able to meet our requirements of educated manpower.

1.8 While these achievements are impressive by themselves, the general formulations incorporated in the 1968 Policy did not, however, get translated into a detailed strategy of implementation, accompanied by the assignment of specific responsibilities and financial and organisational support. As a result, problems of access, quality, quantity, utility and financial outlay, accumulated over the years, have now assumed such massive proportions that they must be tackled with the utmost urgency.

1.9 Education in India stands at the cross roads today. Neither normal linear expansion nor the existing pace and nature of improvement can meet the needs of the situation.

1.10 In the Indian way of thinking, a human being is a positive asset and precious national resource which needs to he cherished, nurtured and developed with tenderness and care, coupled with dynamism. Each individual's growth presents a different range of problems and requirements, at every stage from the womb to the tomb. The catalytic action of education in this complex and dynamic growth process needs to be planned meticulously and executed with great sensitivity.

1.11 India's political and social life is passing through a phase which poses the danger of erosion to long-accepted values. The goals of secularism, socialism, democracy and professional ethics are coming under increasing strain.

1.12 The rural areas, with poor infrastructure and social services, will not get the benefit of trained and educated youth, unless rural-urban disparities are reduced and determined measures are taken to promote diversification and dispersal of employment opportunities.

1.13 The growth of our population needs to be brought down significantly order the coming decades. The largest single factor that could help to achieve this is the spread of literacy and education among women.

1.14 Life in the coming decades is likely to bring new tensions together with unprecedented opportunities. To enable the people to benefit in the new environment will require new designs of human resource development. The coming generations should have the ability to internalise new ideas constantly and creatively. They have to be imbued with a strong commitment to humane values and to social justice. All this implies better education.

1.15 Besides, a variety of new challenges and social needs make it imperative for the Government to formulate and implement a new Education Policy for the country. Nothing short of this will meet the situation.

PART II

THE ESSENCE AND ROLE OF EDUCATION

2.1 In our national perception education is essentially for all. This is fundamental to our all-round development, material and spiritual.

2.2 Education has an acculturating role. It refines sensitivities and perceptions that contribute to national cohesion, a scientific temper and independence of mind and spirit-thus furthering the goals of socialism, secularism and democracy enshrined in our Constitution.

2.3 Education develops manpower for different levels of the economy. It is also the substrata on which research and development flourish, being the ultimate guarantee of national self-reliance.

2.4 In sum, education is a unique investment in the present and file future. This cardinal principle is the key to the National Policy on Education.

PART III

NATIONAL SYSTEM OF EDUCATION

3.1 The Constitution embodies the principles on which the National System of Education is conceived of.

3.2 The concept of a National System of Education implies that, tip to a given level, all students, irrespective of caste, creed, location or sex, have access to education of a comparable quality. To achieve this, the Government will initiate appropriately funded programmes. Effective measures will be taken in the direction of the Common School System recommended in the 1968 policy.

3.3 The National System of Education envisages a common educational structure. The 10+2+3 structure has now been accepted in all parts of the country. Regarding the further break-up of the first 10 years efforts will be made to move towards an elementary system comprising 5 years of primary education and 3 years of upper primary, followed by 2 years of high school.

3.4 The National System of Education will be based on a national curricular framework which contains a common core along with other components that are flexible. The common core will include the history of India's freedom movement, the constitutional obligations and other content essential to nurture national identity. These elements will cut across subject areas and will be designed to promote values such as India's common Cultural heritage, egalitarianism, democracy and secularism, equality of the sexes, protection of the environment, removal of social barriers, observance of the small family norm and inculcation of the scientific temper. All educational programmes will be carried on in strict conformity with secular values.

3.5 India has always worked for peace and understanding between nations, treating the whole world as one family. True to this hoary tradition, Education has to strengthen this world view and motivate the younger generations for international cooperation and peaceful coexistence. This aspect cannot be neglected.

3.6 To promote equality, it will be necessary to provide for equal opportunity to all not only in access, but also in the conditions for success. Besides, awareness of the inherent equality of all will be created through the core curriculum. The purpose is to remove prejudices and complexes transmitted through the social environment and the accident of birth.

3.7 Minimum levels of learning will be laid down for each stage of education. Steps will also be taken to foster among students an understanding of the diverse cultural and social systems of the people living in different parts of the country. Besides the promotion of the link language, programmes will also be launched to increase substantially the translation of books from one language to another and to publish multilingual dictionaries and glossaries. The young will be encouraged to undertake the rediscovery of India, each in his own image and perception.

3.8 In higher education in general, and technical education in particular, steps will be taken to facilitate inter-regional mobility by providing equal access to every Indian of requisite merit, regardless of his origins. The universal character of universities and other institutions of higher education is to be underscored.

3.9 In the areas of research and development, and education in science and technology, special measures will be taken to establish network arrangements between different institutions in the country to pool their resources and participate in projects of national importance.

3.10 The Nation as a whole will assume the responsibility of providing resource support for implementing progra-mmes of educational transformation, reducing disparities, universalisation of elementary education, adult literacy, scientific and technological research, etc.

3.11 Life-long education is a cherished goal of the educational process. This presupposes universal literacy. Opportunities will be provided to the youth, house-wives, agricultural and industrial workers and professionals to continue the education of their choice, at the pace suited to them. The future thrust will be in the direction of open and distance learning.

3.12 The institutions which will be strengthened to play an important role in giving shape to the National

System of Education are the University Grants Commission, the All India Council of Technical Education, the Indian Council of Agricultural Research and the Indian Medical Council. Integrated planning will be instituted among all these bodies so as to establish functional linkages and reinforce programmes of research and postgraduate education. These, together with the National Council of Educational Research and Training, the National Institute of Educational Planning and Administration and the International Institute of Science and Technology Education will be involved in implementing the Education Policy.

A Meaningful Partnership

3.13 The Constitutional Amendment of 1976, which includes Education in the Concurrent List, was a far-reaching step whose implications—substantive, financial and administrative—require a new sharing of responsibility between the Union Government and the State in respect of this vital area of national life. While the role and responsibility of the States in regard to education will remain essentially unchanged, the Union Government would accept a larger responsibility to reinforce the national and integrative character of education, to maintain quality and standards (including those of the teaching profession at all levels), to study and monitor the educational requirements of the country, as a whole in regard to manpower for development, to cater to the needs of research and advanced study, to look after the international aspects of' education, culture and Human Resource

Development and, in general, to promote excellence at all levels of the educational pyramid throughout the country. Concurrency signifies a partnership which is at once meaningful and challenging; the National Policy will be oriented towards giving effect to it in letter and spirit.

PART IV

EDUCATION FOR EQUALITY

Disparities

4.1 The new policy will lay special emphasis on the removal of disparities and to equalise educational opportunity by attending to the specific needs of those who have been denied equality so far.

Education For Women's Equality

4.2 Education will be used as an agent of basic change in the status of women. In order to neutralise the accumulated distortions of the past, there will be a well-conceived edge in favour of women. The National Education System will play a positive, interventionist role in the empowerment of women. It will foster the development of new values through redesigned curricula, textbooks, the training and orientation of teachers, decision-makers and administrators, and the active involvement of educational institutions. This will be an act of faith and social engineering. Women's studies will be promoted as a part of various courses and educational institutions encouraged to take up active programmes to further women's development.

4.3 The removal of women's illiteracy and obstacles inhibiting their access to, and retention in, elementary education will receive overriding priority, through provision of special support services, setting of time targets, and effective monitoring. Major emphasis will be laid on women's participation in vocational, technical and professional education at different levels. The policy of non-discrimination will be pursued vigorously to eliminate sex stereotyping in vocational and professional courses and to promote women's participation in non-traditional occupations, as well as in existing and emergent technologies.

The Education of Scheduled Castes

4.4 The central focus in the SCs' educational development is their equalisation with the non-SC population at all stages and levels of education, in all areas and in all the four dimensions—rural male, rural female, urban male and urban females.

4.5 The measures contemplated for this purpose include:

i) Incentives to indigent families to send their children to school regularly till they reach the age of 14;

ii) Pre-matric scholarship scheme for children of families engaged in occupations such as scavenging, flaying and tanning to be made applicable from Class I onwards. All children of such families, regardless of incomes, will be covered by this scheme and time-bound programmes targeted on them will be undertaken;

iii) Constant micro-planning and verification to ensure that the enrolment, retention and successful completion of courses by SC students do not fall at any stage, and provision of remedial courses to improve their prospects for further education and employment.

iv) Recruitment of teachers from Scheduled Castes;

v) Provision of facilities for SC students in students' hostels at district headquarters, according to a phased programme;

vi) Location of school buildings, Balwadis and Adult Education Centres in such a way as to facilitate full participation of the Scheduled Castes;

vii) The utilisation of NREP and RLEGP resources so as to make substantial educational facilities available to the Scheduled Castes; and

viii) Constant innovation in finding new methods to increase the participation of the Scheduled Castes in the educational process.

The Education of Scheduled Tribes

4.6 The following measures will be taken urgently to bring the Scheduled Tribes on par with others:

i) Priority will be accorded to opening primary schools in tribal areas. The construction of school building will be undertaken in these areas on a priority basis under the normal funds for education, as well as under the NEEP, RLEGP, Tribal Welfare Schemes, etc.

ii) The socio-cultural milieu of the STs has its distinctive characteristics including, in many cases, their own spoken languages. This underlines the need to develop the curricula and devise instructional materials in tribal languages at the initial stages, with arrangements for switching over to the regional language.

iii) Educated and promising Scheduled Tribe youths will be encouraged and trained to take up teaching in tribal areas.

iv) Residential schools, including Ashram Schools, will be established on a large scale.

v) Incentive schemes will be formulated for the Scheduled Tribes, keeping in view their special needs and life styles. Scholarships for higher education will emphasise technical, professional and para-professional courses. Special remedial courses and other programmes to remove psycho-social impediments will be provided to improve their performances in various courses.

vi) Anganwadis, Non-formal and Adult Education Centres will be opened on a priority basis in areas predominantly inhabited by the Scheduled Tribes.

vii) The curriculum at all stages of education will be designed to create an awareness of the rich cultural identity of the tribal people as also of their enormous creative talent.

Other Educationally Backward Sections and Areas

4.7 Suitable incentives will be provided to all educationally backward sections of society, particularly in the rural areas. Hill and desert districts, remote and inaccessible areas and islands will be provided adequate institutional infrastructure.

Minorities

4.8 Some minority groups are educationally deprived or backward. Greater attention will be paid to the education of these groups in the interests of equality and social justice. This will naturally include the Constitutional guarantees given to them to establish and administer their own educational institutions, and protection to their languages and culture. Simultaneously, objectivity will be reflected in the, preparation of textbooks and in all school activities, and all possible measures will be taken to promote an integration based on appreciation of common national goals and ideals, in conformity with the core curriculum.

The Handicapped

4.9 The objective should be to integrate the physically and mentally handicapped with the general community as equal partners, to prepare them for normal growth and to enable them to face life with courage and confidence. The following measures will be taken in this regard:

i) Wherever it is feasible, the education of children with motor handicaps and other mild handicaps will be common with that of others.

ii) Special schools with hostels will be provided, as far as possible at district headquarters, for the severely handicapped children.

iii) Adequate arrangements will be made to give vocational training to the disabled.

iv) Teacher's training programme will be re-oriented, in particular for teachers of primary classes, to deal with the special difficulties of the handicapped children; and

v) Voluntary effort for the education of the disabled will be encouraged in every possible manner.

Adult Education

4.10 Our ancient scriptures define education as that which liberates i.e., provides the instruments for liberation from ignorance and oppression. In the modern world, it would naturally include the ability to read and write, since that is the main instrument of learning. Hence the crucial importance of adult education, including adult literacy.

4.11 The critical development issue today is the continuous upgradation of skills so as to produce manpower resources of the kind and the number required by the society. Since participation by beneficiaries in the development programmes is of crucial importance, systematic programmes of adult education linked with national goals such as alleviation of poverty, national integration, environmental conservation, energisation of the cultural creativity of the people, observance of small family norm, promotion of women's equality, etc. will be organised and the existing programmes reviewed and strengthened.

4.12 The whole nation must pledge itself to the eradication of illiteracy, particularly in the 15-35 age group. The Central and State Governments, political parties and their mass organisations, the mass media and educational institutions must commit themselves to mass literacy programmes of diverse nature. It will also have to involve on a large scale teachers, students, youth, voluntary agencies, employers, etc. Concerted efforts will be made to harness various research agencies to improve the pedagogical aspects of adult literacy. The mass literacy programme would include, in addition to literacy, functional knowledge and skills, and also awareness among learners about the socio-economic reality and the possibility to change it.

4.13 A vast programme of adult and continuing education will be implemented through various ways and channels, including:

a) establishment of centres in rural areas for continuing education;

b) workers' education through the employers, trade unions and concerned agencies of government;

c) post-secondary education institutions;

d) wider promotion of books, libraries and reading rooms;

e) use of radio, TV and films, as mass and group learning media;

f) creation of learners' groups and organisations;

g) programmes of distance learning;

h) organising assistance in self-learning; and

i) organising need and interest-based vocational training programmes.

PART V

REORGANISATION OF EDUCATION AT DIFFERENT STAGES

Early Childhood Care and Education

5.1 The National Policy on Children specially emphasises investment in the development of the young child, particularly children from sections of the population in which first generation learners predominate.

5.2 Recognising the holistic nature of child development, viz., nutrition, health and social, mental, physical, moral and emotional development, Early Childhood Care and Education (ECCE) will receive high priority and be suitably integrated with the Integrated Child Development Services Programme, wherever possible. Day-care centres will be provided as a support service for universalisation of primary education, to enable girls engaged in taking care of siblings to attend school and as a support service for working women belonging to poorer sections.

5.3 Programmes of ECCE will be child-oriented, focused around play and the individuality of the child. Formal methods and introduction of the 3R's will be discouraged at this stage. The local community will be fully involved in these programmes.

5.4 A full integration of child care and pre-primary education will be brought about, both as a feeder and a strengthening factor for primary education and for human resource development in general. In continuation of this stage, the School Health Programme will be strengthened.

Elementary Education

5.5 The new thrust in elementary education will emphasise two aspects: (i) universal enrolment and universal retention of children up to 14 years of age, and (ii) a substantial improvement in the quality of education.

Child-Centred Approach

5.6 A warm, welcoming and encouraging approach, in which all concerned share a solicitude for the needs of the child, is the best motivation for the child to attend school and learn. A child-centred and activity-based process of learning should be adopted at the primary stage. First generation allowed to set their own pace and be given supplementary remedial instruction. As the child grows, the component of cognitive learning will be increased and skills organised through practice. The policy of non-detention at the primary stage will be retained, making evaluation as disaggregated as feasible.

Corporal punishment will be firmly excluded from the educational system and school timings as well as vacations adjusted to the convenience of children.

School Facilities

5.7 Provision will be made of essential facilities in primary schools, including at least two reasonably large rooms that are usable in all weather, and the necessary toys, blackboards, maps, charts, and other learning material. At least two teachers, one of whom a woman, should work in every school, the number increasing as early as possible to one teacher per class. A phased drive, symbolically called Operation Blackboard will be undertaken with immediate effect to improve primary schools all over the country. Government, local bodies, voluntary agencies and individuals will be fully involved. Construction of school buildings will be the first charge on NREP and RLEGP funds.

Non-Formal Education

5.8 A large and systematic programme of non-formal education will be launched for school drop-outs, for children from habitations without schools, working children and girls who cannot attend whole-day schools.

5.9 Modern technological aids will be used to improve the learning environment of NFE centres. Talented and dedicated young men and women from the local community will be chosen to serve as instructors, and particular attention paid to their training. Steps will be taken to facilitate their entry into the formal system in deserving cases. All necessary measures will be taken to ensure that the quality of non-formal education is comparable with formal education.

5.10 Effective steps will be taken to provide a framework for the curriculum on the lines of the national core curriculum, but based on the needs of the learners and related to the local environment. Learning material of high quality will be developed and provided free of charge to all pupils. NFE programmes will provide participatory learning environment, and activities such as games and sports, cultural programmes, excursions, etc.

5.11 Much of the work of running NFE centres will be done through voluntary agencies and panchayati raj institutions. The provision of funds to these agencies will be adequate and timely. The Government will take over-all responsibility for this vital sector.

A Resolve

5.12 The new education policy will give the highest priority to solving the problem of' children dropping out of school and will adopt an array of meticulously formulated strategies based on micro-planning, and applied at the grass-roots level all over the country, to ensure children's retention at school. This effort will be fully coordinated with the network of non-formal education. It shall be ensured that all children who attain the age of about 11 years by 1990 will have had five years of schooling, or its equivalent through the non-formal stream. Likewise, by 1995 all children will be provided free and compulsory education upto 14 years of age.

Secondary Education

5.13 Secondary education begins to expose students to the differentiated roles of science, the humanities and social sciences. This is also an appropriate stage to provide children with a sense of history and national perspective and give them opportunities to understand their constitutional duties and rights as citizens. Conscious internalisation of a healthy work ethos and of the values of a humane and composite culture will be brought about through appropriately formulated curricula. Vocationalisation through specialised institutions or through the refashioning of secondary education can, at this stage, provide valuable manpower for economic growth. Access to secondary education will be widened to cover areas unserved by it at present. In other areas, the main emphasis will be on consolidation.

5.14 It is universally accepted that children with special talent or aptitude should be provided opportunities to proceed at a faster pace, by making good quality education available to them, irrespective of their capacity to pay for it.*

5.15 Pace-setting schools intended to serve this purpose will be established in various parts of the country on a given pattern, but with full scope for innovation and experimentation. Their broad aims will be to serve the objective of excellence, coupled with equity and social justice (with reservation for SCs and STs), to promote national integration by providing opportunities to talented children largely rural, from different parts of the country to live and learn together, to develop their full potential, and, most importantly, to become catalysts of a nation-wide programme of school improvement. The schools will be residential and free of charge.

Vocationalisation

5.16 The introduction of systematic, well-planned and rigorously implemented programmes of vocational education is crucial in the proposed educational reorganisation. These elements are meant to enhance individual employability, to reduce the mismatch between the demand and supply of skilled manpower, and to provide an alternative for those pursuing higher education without particular interest or purpose.

5.17 Vocational education will be a distinct stream, intended to prepare students for identified occupations spanning several areas of activity. These courses will ordinarily be provided after the secondary stage, but keeping the scheme flexible, they may also be made available after Class VIII. In the interests of integrating vocational education better with their facilities the Industrial Training Institutes will also conform to the larger vocational pattern.

5.18 Health planning and health service management should optimally interlock with the education and training of appropriate categories of health manpower through health-related vocational courses. Health education at the primary and middle levels will ensure the commitment of the individual to family and community health, and lead to health-related vocational courses at the +2 stage of higher secondary education. Efforts will be made to devise similar vocational courses based on agriculture, marketing, social services etc. An emphasis in vocational education will also be on development of attitudes, knowledge, and skills for entrepreneurship and sell-employment.

5.19 The establishment of vocational courses or institutions will be the responsibility of the Government as well as employers in the public and private sectors; the Government will, however, take special steps to cater to the needs of women, rural and tribal students and the deprived sections of society. Appropriate programmes will also be started for the handicapped.

5.20 Graduates of vocational courses will be given opportunities, under predetermined conditions, for professional growth, career improvement and lateral entry into courses of general, technical and professional education through appropriate bridge courses.

5.21 Non-formal, flexible and need-based vocational programmes will also be made available to neoliterates, youth who have completed primary education, school drop-outs, persons engaged in work and unemployed or partially employed persons. Special attention in this regard will be given to women.

5.22 Tertiary level courses will be organised for the young who graduate from the higher secondary courses of the academic stream and may also require vocational courses.

5.23 It is proposed that vocational courses cover 10 per cent of higher secondary students by 1990 and 25 per cent by 1995. Steps will be taken to see that a substantial majority of the products of vocational courses are employed or become self-employed. Review of the courses offered would be regularly undertaken. Government will also review its recruitment policy to encourage diversifications at the secondary level.

Higher Education

5.24 Higher education provides people with an opportunity to reflect on the critical social, economic, cultural, moral and spiritual issues facing humanity. It contributes to national development through dissemination of specialised knowledge and skills. It is therefore a crucial factor for survival. Being at the apex of the educational pyramid, it has also a key role in producing teachers for the education system.

5.25 In the context of the unprecedented explosion of knowledge, higher education has to become dynamic as never before, constantly entering uncharted areas.

5.26 There are around 150 universities and about 5,000 colleges in India today. In view of the need to effect an all round improvement in these institutions, it is proposed that, in the near future, the main emphasis will be on the consolidation of, and expansion of facilities in, the existing institutions.

5.27 Urgent steps will be taken to protect the system from degradation.

5.28 In view of mixed experiences with the system of affiliation autonomous colleges will be helped to develop in large numbers until the affiliating system is replaced by a freer and more creative association of universities with colleges. Similarly, the creation of autonomous departments within universities on a selective basis will be encouraged. Autonomy and freedom will be accompanied by accountability.

5.29 Course and programmes will be redesigned to meet the demands of specialisation better. Special emphasis will be laid on linguistic competence. There will be increasing flexibility in the combination of courses.

5.30 State level planning and coordination of higher education will be done through Councils of Higher Education. The UGC and these Councils will develop coordinative methods to keep a watch on standards.

5.31 Provision will be made for minimum facilities and admission will be regulated according to capacity. A major effort will be directed towards the transformation of' teaching methods. Audio-visual aids and electronic equipment will be introduced; development of science and technology curricula and material, research, and teacher orientation will receive attention. This will require preparation of teachers at the beginning of the service as well as continuing education thereafter. Teacher's performance will be systematically assessed. All posts will be filled on the basis of merit.

5.32 Research in the universities will be provided enhanced support and steps will be taken to ensure its high quality. Suitable mechanisms will be set up by the UGC for coordinating research in the universities, particularly in thrust areas of science and technology, with research undertaken by other agencies. An effort will be made to encourage the setting up of national research facilities within the university system, with proper forms of autonomous management.

5.33 Research in Indology, the humanities and social sciences will receive adequate support. To fulfil the need for the synthesis of knowledge, inter-disciplinary research will be encouraged. Efforts will be made to delve into India's ancient fund of knowledge and to relate it to contemporary reality. This effort will imply the development of facilities for the intensive study of Sanskrit and other classical language.

5.40 De-linking will be applied in services university degree need not be a necessary qualification. Its implementation will lead to a re-fashioning of job-specific courses and afford greater justice to those candidates who, despite being equipped for a given job, are unable to get it because of it is unnecessary for graduate candidates.

5.41 Concomitant with de-linking, an appropriate machinery, such as a National Testing Service, will be established, in appropriate phases, to conduct tests on a voluntary basis to determine the suitability of candidates for specified jobs and to pave the way for the emergence of norms of comparable competence across the nation.

PART VI

TECHNICAL AND MANAGEMENT EDUCATION

6.3 In order to improve the situation regarding manpower information, the recently set up Technical

Manpower Information System will be further developed and strengthened.

6.4 Continuing education, covering established as well as emerging technologies, will be promoted.

6.5 As computers have become important and ubiquitous tools, a minimal exposure to computers and a training in their use will form part of professional education. Programmes of computer literacy will be organised on wide scale from the school stage.

6.6 In view of the present rigid entry requirements to formal courses restricting the access of a large segment of people to technical and managerial education, programmes through a distance-learning process, including uses of the mass media, will be offered. Technical and manage-ment education programmes, including education in polytechnics, will also be on a flexible modular pattern based, on credits, with provision for multi-point entry. A strong guidance and counselling service will be provided.

6.7 In order to increase the relevance of management education, particularly in the non-corporate and under-managed sectors, the management education system will study and document the Indian experience and create a body of knowledge and specific educational programmes suited to these sectors.

6.8 Appropriate formal and non-formal programmes of technical education will be devised for the benefit of women, the economically and socially weaker sections, and the physically handicapped.

6.9 The emphasis on vocational education and its expansion will need a large number of teachers and professionals in vocational education, educational technology curriculum development, etc. Programmes will be started to meet this demand.

6.10 To encourage students to consider 'self-employment' as a career option, training in entrepreneurship will be provided through modular of optional courses, in degree or diploma programmes.

6.11 In order to meet the continuing needs of updating curriculum, renewal should systematically phase out obsolescence and introduce new technologies or disciplines.

Institutional Thrusts

6.12 Some polytechnics in the rural areas have started training weaker groups in those areas for productive occupations through a system of community polytechnics. The community polytechnic system will be appraised and appropriately strengthened to increase its quality and coverage.

Innovation, Research and Development

6.13 Research as a means of renovation and renewal of educational processes will be undertaken by all higher technical institutions. It will primarily aim at producing quality manpower capable of taking tip R&D functions. Research for development will focus on improving present technologies, developing new indigenous ones and enhancing production and productivity. A suitable system for watching and forecasting technology will be set up.

6.14 The scope for cooperation, collaboration and networking relationships between institutions at various levels and with the user systems will be utilised. Proper mainte-nance and an attitude of innovation and improvement will be promoted systematically.

Promoting Efficiency and Effectiveness at All Levels

6.15 As technical and management education is expensive, the following major steps will be taken for cost-effectiveness and to promote excellence:

i) High priority will be given to modernisation and removal of obsolescence. However, modernisation will be undertaken to enhance functional efficiency and not for its own sake or as a status symbol;

ii) Institutions will be encouraged to generate resources using their capacities to provide services to the community and industry. They will be equipped with up-to-date learning resources, library and computer facilities;

iii) Adequate hostel accommodation will be provided, specially for girls. Facilities for sports, creative work and cultural activities will be expanded;

iv) More effective procedures will be adopted in the recruitment of staff. Career opportunities, service conditions, consultancy norms and other perquisites will be improved.

v) Teachers will have multiple roles to perform: teaching, research, development of learning resource material, extension, and managing the institution. Initial and in-service training will be made mandatory for faculty members and adequate training reserves will be provided. Staff Development Programmes will be integrated at the State, and coordinated at regional and national levels.

vi) The curricula of technical and management programmes will be targeted on current as well as the projected needs of industry or user system. Active interaction between technical or management institutions and industry will be promoted in programme planning and implementation, exchange of personnel, training facilities and resources, research and consultancy and other areas of mutual interest.

vii) Excellence in performance of institutions and individuals will be recognised and rewarded. The emergence of substandard and institutions will be checked. A climate conducive to excellence and innovation will be promoted with full involvement of the faculty.

viii) Select institutions will be awarded academic administrative and financial autonomy of varying degrees, building in safeguards with respect to accountability.

ix) Networking systems will have to be established between technical education and industry, R&D organisations, programmes of rural and community development, and with other sectors of education with complementary characteristics.

Management Functions and Change

6.16 In view of the likely emergence of changes in management systems and the need to equip students with the ability to cope with them, effective mechanisms will be devised to understand the nature and direction of changes *per se* and to develop the important skill of managing change.

6.17 In view of the integrated nature of the task, the Ministry of Human Resource Development will coordinate the balanced development of engineering, vocational and management education as well as the education of technicians and craftsmen.

6.18 Professional societies will be encouraged and enabled to perform their due role in the advancement of technical and management education.

6.19 The All India Council for Technical Education will be vested with statutory authority for planning, formulation and the maintenance of norms and standards, accreditation, funding of priority areas, monitoring and evaluation, maintaining parity of certification and awards and ensuring the coordinated and integrated development of technical and management education. Mandatory periodic evaluation will be carried out by a duty constituted Accreditation Board.

6.20 In the interests of maintaining standards and for several other valid reasons, the commercialisation of technical and professional education will be curbed. An alternative system will be devised to involve private and voluntary effort in this sector of education, in conformity with accepted norms and goals.

PART VII

MAKING THE SYSTEM WORK

7.1 It is obvious that these and many other new tasks of education cannot be performed in a state of disorder. Education needs to be managed in an atmosphere of utmost intellectual rigour, seriousness of purpose and, at the same time, of freedom essential for innovation and creativity. While far-reaching change will have to be incorporated in the quality and range of education, the process of introducing discipline into the system will have to be started, here and now, in what exists.

7.2 The country has placed boundless trust in the educational system. The people have a right to expect concrete results. The first task is to make it work. All teachers should teach and all students study.

7.3 The strategy in this behalf will consist of:

a) a better deal to teachers with greater accountability;

b) provision of improved student's services and insistence on observance of acceptable norms of behaviour;

c) provision of better facilities to institutions; and

d) creation of a system of performance appraisals of institutions according to standards and norms set at the national or state levels.

PART VIII

REORIENTING THE CONTENT AND PROCESS OF EDUCTION

The Cultural Perspective

8.1 The existing schism between the formal system of education and the country's rich and varied cultural traditions needs to be bridged. The preoccupation with modern technologies cannot be allowed to sever out new generations from the roots in India's history and culture. De-culturisation, de-humanisation and alienation must be avoided at all costs. Education can and must bring about the fine synthesis between change-oriented technologies and the country's continuity of cultural tradition.

8.2 The curricula and processes of education will be enriched by cultural content in as many manifestations as possible. Children will be enabled to develop sensitivity to beauty, harmony and refinement. Resource persons in the community, irrespective of their formal educational qualifications, will be invited to contribute to the cultural enrichment of education, employing both the literate oral traditions of communication. To sustain and carry forward the cultural tradition, the role of old masters, who train pupils through traditional modes will be supported and recognised.

8.3 Linkages will be established between the university system and institutions of higher learning in art, archaeology, oriental studies etc. Due attention will also be paid to the specialised disciplines of fine arts, museology, folklore, etc. Teaching, training and research in these disciplines will be strengthened so as to replenish specialised manpower in them.

Value Education

8.4 The growing concern over the erosion of essential values and an increasing cynicism in society has brought to focus the need for readjustments in the curriculum in order to make education a forceful tool for the cultivation of social and moral values.

8.5 In our culturally plural society, education should foster universal and internal values oriented towards the unity and integration of our people. Such value education should help eliminate obscurantism, religious fanaticism, violence, superstition and fatalism.

8.6 Apart from this combative role, value education has a profound positive content, based on our heritage, national goals universal perceptions. It should lay primary emphasis on this aspect.

Languages

8.7 The education policy of 1968 had examined the question of the development of languages in great detail; its essential provisions can hardly be improved upon and are as relevant today as before. The implementation of this part of the 1968 policy has, however, been uneven. The policy will be implemented more energetically and purposefully.

Books and Libraries

8.8 The availability of books at low prices is indispensable for people's education. Effort will be made to secure easy accessibility to books for all segments of the population. Measures will be taken to improve the quality of books, promote the reading habit and encourage creative writing. Authors' interests will be protected. Good translations of foreign books into Indian languages will be supported. Special attention will be paid to the production of quality books for children, including text books and work books.

8.9 Together with the development of books, a nation-wide movement for the improvement of existing libraries and the establishment of new ones will be taken up. Provision will be made in all educational institutions for library facilities and the status of librarians improved.

Media and Educational Technology

8.10 Modern communication technologies have the potential to bypass several stages and sequences in the process of development encountered in earlier decades. Both the constraints of time and distance at once become manageable. In order to avoid structural dualism, modern educational technology must reach out to the most distant areas and the most deprived sections of beneficiaries simultaneously with the areas of comparative affluence and ready availability.

8.11 Educational technology will be employed in the spread of useful information, the training and re-training of teachers, to improve quality, sharpen awareness of art and culture, inculcate abiding values, etc., both in the formal and non-formal sectors. Maximum use will be made of the available infrastructure. In villages without electricity, batteries or solar packs will be used to run the programme.

8.12 The generation of relevant and culturally compatible educational programmes will form an important component of educational technology, and all available resources in the country will be utilised for this purpose.

8.13 The media have a profound influence on the minds of children as well as adults; some of them tend to encourage consumerism, violence, etc., and have a deleterious effect. Radio and TV programmes which clearly militate against proper educational objectives will be prevented. Steps will be taken to discourage such trends in films and other media also. An active movement will be started to promote the production of children's films of high quality and usefulness.

Work Experience

8.14 Work experience, viewed as purposive and meaningful manual work, organised as an integral part of the learning process and resulting in either goods or services useful to the community, is considered as an essential component at all stages of education, to be provided through well-structured and graded programmes. It would comprise activities in accord with the interests, abilities and needs of students, the level of skills and knowledge to be upgraded with the stages of education. This experience would be helpful on his entry into the workforce. Pre-vocational programmes provided at the lower secondary stage will also facilitate the choice of the vocational courses at the higher secondary stage.

Education and Environment

8.15 There is a paramount need to create a consciousness of the environment. It must permeate all ages and all sections of society, beginning with the child. Environmental consciousness should inform teaching in schools and colleges. This aspect will be integrated in the entire educational process.

Mathematics Teaching

8.16 Mathematics should be visualised as the vehicle to train a child to think, reason, analyse and to articulate logically. Apart from being a specific subject, it should be treated as a concomitant to any subject involving analysis and reasoning.

8.17 With the recent introduction of computers in schools, educational computing and the emergence of learning through the understanding of cause-effect relationships and the interplay of variables, the teaching of mathematics will be suitably redesigned to bring it in line with modern technological devices.

Science Education

8.18 Science education will be strengthened so as to develop in the child well defined abilities and values such as the spirit of inquiry, creativity, objectivity, the courage to question, and an aesthetic sensibility.

8.19 Science education programmes will be designed to enable the learner to acquire problem-solving and decision-making skills and to discover the relationship of science with health, agriculture, industry and other aspects of daily life. Every effort will be made to extend science education to the vast numbers who have remained outside the pale of formal education.

Sports and Physical Education

8.20 Sports and physical education are an integral part of the learning process, and will be included in the evaluation of performance. A nation-wide infrastructure for physical education, sports and games will be built into the educational edifice.

8.21 The infrastructure will consist of playfields, equipment, coaches and teachers of physical education as part of the school improvement programme. Available open spaces in urban areas will be reserved for playgrounds, if necessary by legislation. Efforts will be made to establish sports institutions and hostels where specialised attention will be given to sports activities and sports-related studies, along with normal education. Appropriate encouragement will be given to those talented in sport and games. Due stress will be laid on indigenous traditional games. As a system which promotes an integrated development of body and mind, yoga will receive special attention. Efforts will be made to introduce yoga in all schools; to this end, it will be introduced in teacher training courses.

The Role of Youth

8.22 Opportunities will be provided for the youth to involve themselves in national and social development through educational institutions and outside them. Students will be required to participate in one or the other of existing schemes, namely, the National Service Scheme, National Cadet Corps, etc. Outside the institutions, the youth will be encouraged to take up programmes of development, reform and extension. The National Service Volunteer Scheme will be strengthened.

The Evaluation Process and Examination Reform

8.23 Assessment of performance is an integral part of any process of learning and teaching. As part of sound educational strategy, examinations should be employed to bring about qualitative improvements in education.

8.24 The objective will be to re-cast the examination system so as to ensure a method of assessment that is a valid and reliable measure of student development and a powerful instrument for improving teaching and learning. In functional terms, this would mean:

i) The elimination of excessive element of chance and subjectivity;

ii) The de-emphasis of memorisation;

iii) Continuous and comprehensive evaluation that incorporates both scholastic and non-scholastic aspects of education, spread over the total span of instructional time;

iv) Effective use of the evaluation process by teachers, students and parents:

v) Improvement in the conduct of examinations;

vi) The introduction of concomitant changes in instructional materials and methodology;

vii) Introduction of the semester system from the secondary stage in a phased manner; and

viii) The use of grades in place of marks.

8.25 The above goals are relevant both for external examinations and evaluation within educational institutions. Evaluation at the institutional level will be streamlined and the predominance of external examinations reduced.

PART IX

THE TEACHER

9.1 The status of the teacher reflects the socio-cultural ethos of a society; it is said that no people can rise above the level of its teachers. The Government and the community should endeavour to create conditions which will help motivate and inspire teachers on constructive and creative lines. Teachers should have the freedom to innovate, to devise appropriate methods of communication and activities relevant to the needs and capabilities of and the concerns of the community.

9.2 The methods of recruiting teachers will be reorganised to ensure merit, objectivity and conformity with spatial and functional requirements. The pay and service conditions of teachers have to be commensurate with their social and professional responsibilities and with the need to attract talent to the profession. Efforts will be made to reach the desirable objective of uniform emoluments, service conditions and grievance-removal mechanisms for throughout the country. Guidelines will be formulated to ensure objectivity in the postings and transfers of teachers. A system of teacher evaluation—open, participative and data-based—will be created and reasonable opportunities of promotion to higher grades provided. Norms of accountability will be laid down with incentives for good performance and disincentives for non-performance. Teachers will continue to play a crucial role in the formulation and implementation of educational programmes.

9.3 Teachers' associations must play a significant role in upholding professional integrity, enhancing the dignity of the teacher and in curbing professional misconduct. National level associations of teachers, could prepare a Code of Professional Ethics for Teachers and see to its observance.

Teacher Education

9.4 Teacher education is a continuous process, and its pre-service and in-service components are inseparable. As the first step, the system of teacher education will be overhauled.

9.5 The new programmes of teacher-education will emphasise continuing education and the need for teachers to meet the thrusts envisaged in this policy.

9.6 District. Institutes of Education and Training (DIET) will be established with the capability to organise pre-service and in-service courses for elementary school teachers and for the personnel working in non-formal and adult education. As DIETs get established, substandard institutions will be phased out. Selected Secondary Teacher Training Colleges will be upgraded to complement the work of State Councils of Educational Research and Training. The National Council of Teacher Education will be provided the necessary resources and capability to accredit institutions of teacher-education and provide guidance regarding curricula and methods. Networking arrangements will be created between institutions of teacher education and university depart-ments of education.

PART X

THE MANAGEMENT OF EDUCATION

10.1 An overhaul of the system of planning and the management of education will receive high priority. The guiding considerations will be:

a) Evolving a long-term planning and management perspective of education and its integration with the country's developmental and manpower needs;

b) Decentralisation and the creation of a spirit of autonomy for educational institutions;

c) Giving pre-eminence to people's involvement, including association of non-governmental agencies and voluntary effort;

d) Inducting more women in the planning and manage-ment of education; and

e) Establishing the principle of accountability in relation to given objectives and norms.

National Level

10.2 The Central Advisory Board of Education will play a pivotal rote in reviewing educational development, determining the changes required to improve the system and monitoring implementation. It will function through appropriate committees and other mechanisms created to ensure contact with, and co-ordination among, the various areas of human resource development. The departments of education at the centre and in the states will be strengthened through the involvement of professionals.

Indian Education Service

10.3 A proper management structure in education will entail the establishment of the Indian Education Service as an All-India Service. It will bring a national perspective to this vital sector. The basic principles, functions and procedures of recruitment to this service will be decided in consultation with the State Governments.

State Level

10.4 State Governments may establish State Advisory Boards of Education on the lines of CABE. Effective measures should be taken to integrate mechanisms in the various State departments concerned with Human Resource Development.

10.5 Special attention will be paid to the training of educational planners, administrators and heads of institutions. Institutional arrangements for this purpose should be set up in stages.

District and Local Level

10.6 District Boards of Education will be created to manage education up to the higher secondary level. State Governments will attend to this aspect with all possible expedition. Within a multi-level framework of educat-ional development, central, state, district and local level agencies will participate in planning, coordination, monitoring and evaluation.

10.7 A very important role must be assigned to the head of an educational institution. Heads will be specially selected and trained. School complexes will be promoted on a flexible pattern so as to serve as networks of institutions and synergic alliances to encourage professionalism among teachers, to ensure observance of norms of conduct and to enable the sharing of experiences and facilities. It is expected that a developed system of school complexes will take much of the inspection functions in due course.

10.8 Local communities, through appropriate bodies, will be assigned a major role in programmes of school improvement.

Voluntary Agencies and Aided Institutions

10.9 Non-government and voluntary effort including social activist groups will be encouraged, subject to proper management, and financial assistance provided. At the same time, steps will be taken to prevent the establis-hment of institutions set up to commercialise education.

PART XI

RESOURCES AND REVIEW

11.1 The Education Commission of 1964-66, the National Education Policy of 1968 and practically all others concerned with education have stressed that the egalitarian goals and the practical, development-oriented objectives of Indian society can be realised only by making investments in education of an order comme-nsurate with the nature and dimensions of the task.

11.2 Resources, to the extent possible, will be raised by mobilising donations, asking the beneficiary communities to maintain school buildings and supplies of some consumables, raising fees at the higher levels of education and effecting some savings by the efficient use of facilities. Institutions involved with research and the development of technical and scientific manpower should also mobilise some funds by levying access or charge on the user agencies, including government departments, and entrepreneurs. All these measures will be taken not only to reduce the burden on State resources but also for creating a greater sense of responsibility within the educational system. However, such measures will contribute only marginally to the total funding. The government and the community in general will find funds for such programmes as: the universalisation of elementary education; liquidating illiteracy; equality of access to educational opportunities to all sections throughout the country; enhancing the social relevance, quality and functional effectiveness of educational programmes; generating knowledge and developing technologies in scientific fields crucial to self-sustaining economic development; and creating a critical consciousness of the values and imperatives of national survival.

11.3 The deleterious consequences of non-investment or inadequate investment in education are indeed very serious. Similarly, the cost of neglecting vocational and technical education and of research is also unacceptable. Sub-optimal performance in these fields could cause irreparable damage to the Indian economy. The network of institutions set up from time to time since independence to facilitate the application of science and technology would need to be substantially and expeditiously updated, since they are fast becoming obsolete.

11.4 In view of these imperatives, education will be treated as a crucial area of investment for national development and survival. The National Policy on Education, 1968, had laid down that the investment on education be gradually increased to reach a level of expenditure of 6 per cent of the national income as early as possible. Since the actual level of investment has remained far short of that target, it is important that greater determination be shown now to find the funds for the programmes laid down in this policy. While the actual requirements will be computed from time to time on the basis of monitoring and review, the outlay on education will be shaped up to the extent essential for policy implementation in the Seventh Plan. It will be ensured that from the Eighth Five Year Plan onwards it will uniformly exceed to 6 per cent of the national income.

Review

11.5 The implementation of the various parameters of the new policy must be reviewed every five years. Appraisals at short intervals will also be made to ascertain the progress of implementation and the trends emerging from time to time.

PART XII

THE FUTURE

12.1 The future of education in India is too complex to envision with precision. Yet, given our tradition which has almost always put a high premium on intellectual and spiritual attainment, we are bound to succeed in achieving our objectives.

12.2 The main tasks is to strengthen the base of the pyramid, which might come close to a billion people at the turn of the century. Equally, it is important to ensure that those at the top of the pyramid are among the best in the world. Our cultural wellsprings had taken good care of both ends in the past; the skew set in with foreign domination and influence. It should now be possible to further intensify the nation-wide effort in Human Resource Development, with education playing its multifaceted role.

Bibliography

Biswas A and Aggarwal, S.P., *Development of Education in India: A Historical Survey of Educational Documents before and after Independence,* New Delhi, Concept Publishing Co., 1986.

Burge, E., 1993, "Adult Distance Learning: Challenges for Contemporary Practice", In Thelma Barer-Stein and James A. Draper (eds.), *The Craft of Teaching Adults,* Toronto, Ontario: Culture Concepts, pp. 131-144.

Chandrsekaran P., 1994, *Educational Planning and Management,* Sterling Publishers (P) Ltd., New Delhi.

Comeaux, P., 1995, "The Impact of an Interactive Distance Learning Network on Classroom Communication", *Communication Education,* 41(4), pp. 353-361.

Dahama, O. P., and Bhatnagar, O. P., 1988, *Education and Communication for Development,* Oxford and IBH Publishing Co. Pvt. Ltd.

Galusha, J. M., 1998, *Barriers to Learning in Distance Education, Interpersonal Computing and Technology,* 5(3-4), pp. 6-14.

Goel, S.L., Goel, A., 1994, *Education Policy and Administration,* Deep and Deep Publications, New Delhi.

Government of India (1966), *Report on the Education Commission 1964-66): Education and National Development,* GOI, New Delhi.

Hodgkinson, C., 1991, *Educational Leadership: The Moral Art,* Albany, NY: State University of New York Press.

Kelly, M. J. 1999. In: *Learning Opportunities for All: A Policy Framework for Education.* UK Department for International Development.

Mezirow, J (1991) *Transformative Dimensions of Adult Learning,* Jossey-

Bass Publishers, San Francisco MHRD, New Delhi..

Ministry of Human Resources Development. *National policy on Education.* New Delhi, Government of India, 1993.

Mukhopadhyay, B., 1994, *Motivation in Education Management, Issues and Strategies,* Sterling Publishers Pvt. Ltd., New Delhi.

Noddings, A., 1992, *The Challenge to Care in Schools: An Alternative Approach to Education,* New York: Teachers College Press.

Ochp, L.O., 1978. "*A Model for Participative Decision-Making in Secondary Schools*", Unpublished Ph.D. Thesis, Cordiff: University of Wales.

Report of the committee for review of NPE, 1986, "Towards and Enlightened and Human Society", *NPE, 1986—A Review,* (Final Report), Dec. 1990.

Singh, Rajendra Prasad, 1997, *Educational Finance and the Planning Challenge,* Kanishka Publishers, New Delhi.

Stringer, W., 1992, "Education Policy, National Curriculum and Schools", In Stockley, D., (ed.), *Rationalising Education,* Melbourne: Melbourne Studies in Education, Latrobe University Press.

Index